PRAISE FOR *FINDING THE GOOD*

"Our divided nation and the world are in desperate need of healing. Hate divides us, but forgiveness makes room for reconciliation and understanding. My father wrote, 'There is some good in the worst of us and some evil in the best of us. When we discover this, we are less prone to hate our enemies.' *Finding the Good* is a captivating story about the extraordinary life of a man who made this discovery and the transformative domino effect that the healing power of forgiveness and love made in his life and in the lives of those he encountered."

—Dr. Bernice A. King, CEO, The King Center

"It's important that everybody reads this book, to get on the same page, for our mutual salvation."

—Louis Gossett Jr., Academy Award–winning actor who won an Emmy for his role in the miniseries *Roots*

"Deeply touching. I will cherish it for a long time to come."

—Desmond Tutu, Nobel Peace Prize laureate

"Gingerbread, fried chicken, homemade ice cream, *Finding the Good*, reaffirming life, struggle, peace, satisfaction—yeah!"

—Nikki Giovanni, acclaimed poet, activist, and educator

"As our country grapples with race relations as never before, *Finding the Good* destroys stereotypes, shatters excuses, and opens the door for national dialogue. All of us have a chance to display what can happen when love leads the conversation. Enjoy the read. Imagine what is possible. And muster the courage to care!"

—T. D. Jakes, multi-bestselling author, filmmaker, and senior pastor at the Potter's House of Dallas

"Fred Montgomery symbolizes and embodies the greatest generation of people in the USA. The generation who fought daily to claim their humanity and to resist a century of racism, clinging to the promises of the promised land. I strongly recommend this book!"

—Rev. James M. Lawson Jr., emeritus pastor and leading
tactician of nonviolence within the civil rights movement

"*Finding the Good* is a well-written, highly inspirational story of African American Tennessean Fred Montgomery, who happened to be Alex Haley's best friend in the village of Henning, in the western part of that state. Montgomery befriended the young journalist Lucas Johnson, who recounts Montgomery's story and explores his Christian faith. Along the way, Johnson reveals the character and philosophy of Alex Haley through Montgomery's recollections. This book is a life-affirming opportunity on many levels."

—Robert J. Norrell, author of *Alex Haley: And
the Books That Changed a Nation*

"*Finding the Good* shows us just how much representation, hope, and dreams of racial equity matter. The life lessons revealed in this insightful work give all Americans, regardless of race, a chance to see the redemptive power of grace at work."

—Jennifer Woodard, diversity and inclusion expert and assistant
dean at MTSU College of Media and Entertainment

"*Finding the Good* is a vulnerable compare-and-contrast story that illustrates a counterintuitive approach to resolving race relations in America. While many have become discouraged by the bad and the unfortunate, Johnson highlights the bravery of Mr. Montgomery, a Black man who musters the fortitude to find the good in the heart of the Jim Crow South. This text is exactly what America needs right now! And Lucas Johnson is the type of author who can bring a calming peace to our national storm."

—Michael A. Polite, human development specialist

"*Finding the Good* is a composition of inspiration, motivation, and belief that no matter how bad the majority of people may seem, good people still exist!"

—Chris Blue, singer, songwriter, and season 12–winner of *The Voice*

"Mr. Montgomery is an American treasure. His life is a shining example of how love prevails over hate and transcends into the spirit of forgiveness. *Finding the Good* is a catalyst for self-reflection, healing, and change."

—Karla L. Winfrey, Emmy-winning multimedia journalist

"I have dedicated my life to serving youth and young adults—providing vital exposure, creating opportunities to gain critical skills, and helping each student embrace the good in their life—and I truly believe this is a generational story that needs to be told. Exposure, knowledge, and positivity are essential for any youth attempting to transition through life, which is why this book is so important. I'm both glad and grateful that Lucas Johnson has made this happen."

—Keith Strickland, founder and CEO of Making the Transition

"Those who read *Finding the Good* will be better people—better neighbors, better brothers and sisters, better sons and daughters, better mothers and fathers, better friends—because of it."

—Will Rodgers, award-winning communicator and entrepreneur

"It isn't often that a book is as inspiring as this one."

—Dennie Hall, book editor for *The Oklahoman*

FINDING THE GOOD

**TWO MEN—ONE OLD, ONE YOUNG—FOREVER CHANGED BY
THE TRANSFORMING POWER OF FORGIVENESS AND LOVE**

LUCAS L. JOHNSON II

NELSON
BOOKS

An Imprint of Thomas Nelson

Published in Nashville, Tennessee, by Nelson Books, an imprint of Thomas Nelson. Nelson Books and Thomas Nelson are registered trademarks of HarperCollins Christian Publishing, Inc.

Thomas Nelson titles may be purchased in bulk for educational, business, fundraising, or sales promotional use. For information, please e-mail SpecialMarkets@ThomasNelson.com.

Unless otherwise noted, Scripture quotations taken from The Holy Bible, New International Version®, NIV®. Copyright © 1973, 1978, 1984, 2011 by Biblica, Inc.® Used by permission of Zondervan. All rights reserved worldwide. www.Zondervan.com. The "NIV" and "New International Version" are trademarks registered in the United States Patent and Trademark Office by Biblica, Inc.®

Scripture quotations marked NKJV are taken from the New King James Version®. Copyright © 1982 by Thomas Nelson. Used by permission. All rights reserved.

Any internet addresses, phone numbers, or company or product information printed in this book are offered as a resource and are not intended in any way to be or to imply an endorsement by Thomas Nelson, nor does Thomas Nelson vouch for the existence, content, or services of these sites, phone numbers, companies, or products beyond the life of this book.

ISBN: 978-1-4002-3160-7 (Repack)
ISBN: 978-1-4185-3078-5 (eBook)
ISBN: 978-1-4016-0074-7 (TP)

Library of Congress Cataloging-in-Publication Data

Johnson, Lucas, 1969–
Finding the good / by Lucas Johnson.
p. cm
ISBN 978-1-4016-0037-9 (hardcover)
1. Montgomery, Fred, 1916– 2. African Americans – Tennessee – Henning – Biography.
    3. Historians – Tennessee - Henning – Biography. 4. Mayors – Tennessee - Henning – Biography. 5. Henning (Tenn.)—Biography. 6. Henning (Tenn.)—Race relations. 7. African Americans – Tennessee – Henning – Social conditions—20th century. 8. Haley, Alex – Friends and associates. 9. Haley, Alex – Homes and haunts – Tennessee – Henning. 10. Johnson, Lucas, 1969– I. Title.
F444.H44J64 2003
976.8'16—dc21   2003007752

Printed in the United States of America
21 22 23 24 25 LSC 10 9 8 7 6 5 4 3 2 1

This book is dedicated to my grandmother,
Gladys Johnson,
and in memory of her husband,
my grandfather, Leroy.

CONTENTS

FOREWORD

On January 21, 2013, speaking from the East Front of the US Capitol to nearly a million people watching President Barack Obama's second inauguration, I quoted a man from Henning, Tennessee:

> The late Alex Haley, the author of *Roots*, lived his life by these six words: find the good and praise it.
>
> Today we praise the American tradition of transferring or reaffirming immense power as we inaugurate the President of the United States. We do this in a peaceful, orderly way. There is no mob. No coup. No insurrection. This is a moment when millions stop and watch. A moment most of us always will remember. It is a moment that is our most conspicuous and enduring symbol of the American democracy.
>
> How remarkable that this has survived for so long in such a complex country when so much power is at stake. This freedom to vote for our leaders and the restraint to respect the results.

Last year, a tour guide at Mt. Vernon told me that our first president, George Washington, posed this question: "What is most important of this grand experiment, the United States?"

And then Washington gave this answer: "Not the election of the first president, but the election of its second president. The peaceful transition of power is what will separate this country from every other country in the world."

Today we celebrate, because this is the 57th inauguration of the American President.[1]

"Find the good and praise it," I concluded, repeating Haley's motto once more.

Alex Haley may be Henning's most famous son, but his best boyhood friend, Fred Montgomery, was an equally steady force of wisdom. Fred and Alex grew up in homes three blocks apart. Although their great-grandparents were born into slavery, Fred became mayor of Henning and Alex won the Pulitzer Prize.

It's a pretty remarkable message coming from two men who grew up African American in the South during the 1920s. What Lucas Johnson has captured in this book is the resilient optimism of these two men—their hope for themselves and their hope for our country.

One prayer that Fred prayed has stuck with me for a long time. It was on July 4, 1994, and I was beginning an 8,800-mile drive across America with an overnight stay in Fred's guest room. I was also in the midst of deciding whether or not to run for president in 1996.

Fred and I began the evening by meeting with local officials and others convened in the city hall, where talk of the town's first drive-by shooting led to a discussion not about the pending federal crime legislation but about ways to encourage better parenting and more local control. And then we headed for a fish fry of crappie that Mayor Montgomery and his family had caught and cooked.

Fred had said a blessing that evening before we ate our supper:

> No matter how your ancestors arrived here, no matter what color your skin, no matter what language your grandparents spoke, we are all here. We are all Americans. And with all her faults, America is still the greatest place in the world to live. Cherish your country. Cherish your freedom and hold on to your dreams.

Before going to sleep that night, I stashed in a safe place the scrap of paper on which I had scribbled those words.

Faith is a theme that resonates throughout Johnson's book. I experienced, firsthand, the stabilizing force of Fred Montgomery's faith. In 1993, Fred talked a little about prayer with my son, Will, when we stopped for a visit in Henning. Standing in the Haley Museum, Fred told Will about how he and Alex grew up. "At 9:00 p.m., in every black home in Henning with which I was familiar," Fred said, "we went down on our knees in prayer, because we believed that somehow our prayers would be lifted up into the clouds and that tomorrow would be better than today."

At a time of political turmoil, social-media cynicism, and the fight against a deadly global pandemic, this book is a timely reminder that any one of us can have optimism for our own lives, for our communities, and for our nation—even in the face of real difficulty and hardship.

If Fred Montgomery and Alex Haley can "find the good" and believe that tomorrow will be better than today, surely, we can too.

LAMAR ALEXANDER

INTRODUCTION

Darkness cannot drive out darkness;
only light can do that.
Hate cannot drive out hate; only love can do that.
—MARTIN LUTHER KING JR.

I n spring 1996, I got the freelance assignment. It was a slow news day at the Nashville, Tennessee, Associated Press bureau, and I was shooting the breeze with a coworker, Joe Edwards. A friendly, easygoing guy, Joe seemed always to have my best interests at heart, and I kind of looked up to him. After all, he'd been at the AP for more than thirty years, longer than anyone on the editorial staff. He could have been chief of bureau somewhere if he wanted. But knowing Joe, he just didn't want the headache. He liked things steady and routine—to go home to his lovely wife, Sandra, and their dog, Emmitt.

On this particular day, Joe told me he'd received a call from one of his contacts at the Tennessee Tourism Department about a national tourism magazine that was looking for someone to do a feature story on the Alex Haley Museum in Henning. He thought the assignment would be perfect for me and gave me the magazine contact. Shamefully, I must admit I'd never heard of the museum, but I did know Haley was from Henning. When I talked to the editor at *Friendly Exchange*, she gave me details about the assignment and told me I might want to pay close attention to the museum's curator. That's all she said about him. At the time, I didn't care to know too much more, except maybe how much I was getting paid.

Henning, located about fifty miles north of Memphis, has a population of roughly twelve hundred that is about 60 percent black. Near Henning are Covington and Ripley, two slightly larger towns. As a child, I remember going to a Methodist church in Covington when my mother's denomination had youth conferences during the summer. But I had no idea what was beyond Covington. Needless to say, on my way to Henning for the assignment, I was reminded of the meandering country roads we had to travel. As I turned each curve, I thought about my childhood and the bumps I encountered.

I was raised in a rough part of Memphis, called Orange Mound. The neighborhood wasn't that bad when we moved there in 1969. But like many black communities in the late seventies and early eighties, it grew progressively worse as cocaine came on the drug scene. Dope houses began to crop up on both sides of my street, and drug dealers were the entrepreneurs of the community. As violence grew within its borders, Orange Mound became notorious in the South, much like Los Angeles's Compton. My friends embraced its tough reputation. Most of them were fatherless, and they dreamed of emulating the lifestyle of the dealers who kept rolls of hundreds in their pockets and drove flashy cars. Still boys, they chose the path they thought led to manhood.

My mother, Shirley, is a petite, hardworking woman who almost single-handedly raised my two older sisters and me. She did her best to shelter me. She walked me to the bus stop nearly every day till she thought I was big enough to take care of myself. Even though she had only a high school diploma, my mother had a PhD in sewing. She worked at that machine sometimes from sunup to sundown to help provide for us.

My father, Lucas, after whom I'm named, also worked diligently. After high school, he went to work for a Jewish dry cleaner named Kalman for a number of years, until a close friend suggested he consider teaching dry cleaning at a local high school. At age thirty-seven, my father went to night school to get a bachelor's degree in education and taught during the day. He was tenacious and made a pretty good salary at what he did. He helped my mother pay the bills and made sure there was plenty to eat. But he had a serious problem. His finances and health were often strained by two abusive friends: Jack Daniel's and Crown Royal. You see, my father was also an alcoholic. He was sort of a Dr. Jekyll and Mr. Hyde. Throughout the week he was a teacher, but on weekends he was "the world's worst," a phrase I often heard him mumble to himself as he staggered into the house and collapsed on the bed.

Those were heart-wrenching times for me. Sometimes I didn't think my father would make it through the night. I remember one evening he was so intoxicated that he had to crawl to the bed. I was sure he was going to die. At age ten, I remember hopping out of my bed and tiptoeing to his bedroom to make sure he was still breathing. I did this several times throughout the night, until I eventually tired myself out and drifted off to sleep. I begged him to stop drinking many times. He always promised he would, and for a while I would be optimistic. But too many broken promises can lead to hopelessness, even tears. And I shed many.

If I wasn't smelling alcohol, then it was marijuana. I often watched with wide-eyed curiosity as my older cousins and their friends rolled joints and smoked until their eyes turned bloodshot, while Jimi Hendrix's "Purple Haze" played in the background. As curious as I was about their euphoric state, I never asked to take a drag, nor did they let me. Instead, they practiced tossing me like a ball from one to the other and body-slamming me onto the bed. They said it was a way of toughening me up, of making a man out of me. They claimed the sheltering my mother gave me was going to make me a sissy. In their own way, they were showing me tough love, and their rough-and-tumble nurturing did play a part in my growth into manhood. But I didn't really know what being a man was about until I visited my father's father, Leroy, the man we all knew as Daddy Roy.

My grandfather was a calm, gentle man. He had a farm in Collierville, just outside of Memphis. When my father wasn't drinking, my mother would let me go with him to visit my grandfather. Dark-skinned, and standing about five feet eight, Daddy Roy exuded a deep, quiet strength, like the deceptively strong waters of the Tennessee River. He and my grandmother Gladys had four girls and three sons, one stillborn. Every time I saw them together, they always seemed to get along, never arguing. She respected him and he respected her. I remember Daddy Roy telling me one time that my grandmother did get on his nerves sometimes (I'm sure he got on hers too), but never to the point that he thought about raising his hand to her or calling her a bad name.

It wasn't just my grandmother who respected Daddy Roy. He also garnered respect from those who knew him. I know my own respect for him was enormous. If he had ever frowned at me, I probably would have crumbled. But he never did. He always smiled. During one visit I accidentally locked myself in the bathroom. My grandmother fussed a bit, but Daddy Roy took me outside and simply told me to be more careful. He then patted me on the back, and everything was okay in the world. He had a way of doing that, of making me feel special.

I was a short, big-eyed kid, barely weighing a buck-o-five. Mickey Mouse and I could have been brothers. But even though I was small, I always wanted to hang with the big boys. And when it came to work, I tried to show that I was just as strong as them. Sometimes I would go with my father to help Daddy Roy during hay-baling season. One day I decided I was going to do more than just look. I grabbed a bale of hay that was almost bigger than me. It took all I had, but I managed to lift it onto the back of the trailer. My grandfather apparently saw my display of herculean prowess and later called out as he stood over several bales: "Where's that stout boy?" Words can't describe how large I felt at that moment. *I can do anything*, I thought, *if I just put my mind to it*.

I didn't quite understand how my grandfather maintained his peaceful personality, until I was walking outside one day and stumbled across him sitting under a shade tree. His eyes were closed, and he seemed to be mumbling something. I thought he was talking to himself. But as I stood there and listened, I occasionally heard him whisper the name Jesus. He was praying.

In summer 1995, prostate cancer took him away at age eighty-five. I was twenty-five then. Even though he had been sick for a while and the family expected him to go at any time, his final departure was still tough, especially for me. However, I had a dream a short time after his death that comforted me. I was standing outside my grandparents' house when an angel appeared and told me Daddy Roy was going to be all right, but that if I wanted to see him again, "You've got to make sure your life is together." I'd always heard that God works in mysterious ways. And when I look back, I truly believe he sent a surrogate to Henning to help me get my life together.

When I got about five miles outside Covington, I saw the sign that read: Henning, Home of Alex Haley. About a mile from the interstate was the Henning city limits, and a mile from that was another sign pointing in the direction of the museum. As I drove through the small town square and down the street to my destination, the buildings and old homes reminded me of those I'd seen in books about the Old South. There were the large frame houses with their columns and spacious porches decorated with flowers and rocking chairs. Then there were the shotgun houses, which signified the town was once divided between blacks and whites, as was common in most rural southern towns. When I reached my destination, I was surprised. I expected a building or a large plantation-style house. But the Alex Haley Museum was neither. It was a bluish bungalow-style home that had been turned into a museum. In a way, I was a little disappointed.

After a few knocks on the back-porch screen door, a short, older black man appeared. "Hi. My name's Fred Montgomery. Come on in," he said in a calm yet clear voice. He was up in age, but his pace wasn't slow. It was rather quick and short, as if he were certain of every direction. I could tell he was of some Native American descent. His hair was silver gray and his skin was bronze. Large-framed glasses sat on his long, narrow face, and for a moment, he sort of resembled a judge or a college professor I once knew. When he talked, the peacefulness in his voice reminded me of Daddy Roy.

I told Mr. Montgomery my assignment, and he said the best way to learn about the house was to take a tour. He proceeded to tell me that he was not only the curator of the museum but the mayor of Henning. He and Alex Haley were boyhood friends and later traveled together when Haley was writing the book *Roots*. He said Haley was able to trace his family history back seven generations to his great-great-great-great-grandfather Kunta Kinte from stories he'd heard on the front porch of his grandparents' house. The book eventually won a Pulitzer Prize, and it was turned into an eight-part miniseries that aired in the winter of 1977 and was watched by more than 130 million viewers.

I was seven years old at the time and didn't fully understand what I was seeing. But the images and sounds were disturbing nonetheless—people who looked like me tightly packed in the belly of a ship, lying in their own filthy waste for months; mothers wailing over the loss of children they'd never see again; bloody backs and rotting bodies.

Haley took the horrific images of the Middle Passage and placed them in the living rooms across America. Because of the enormous interest it drew, the networks began showing the miniseries just about every year. Occasionally, they would also air the follow-up, *Roots: The Next Generations*, which was made about two years later. When I was in my late twenties, I saw the original miniseries from beginning to end as well as the follow-up series. From watching them I learned about noble values and saw grit and strong moral character that stuck with me, almost as if they were preparing me for something.

At one point of the tour, Mr. Montgomery pointed to a picture of Haley hanging on the wall inside the doorway of the museum. He was standing on a dock, looking out across what appeared to be a large body of water. Mr. Montgomery said it was where Haley believed the first slave ships arrived in America. He told Mr. Montgomery that if he was still enough, he could almost hear the wails of the millions of slaves who died during the Middle Passage and see them coming onto the dock in chains, some bloody from being beaten, others near starvation.

As we walked through the museum, Mr. Montgomery pointed to a picture directly on the wall in front of me. It was of an old African woman, and her piercing eyes seemed to be staring right at me. Her name was Binter Kinte, the sixth cousin of Kunta Kinte, whose descendants Haley sought in Gambia to learn more about his ancestors. Mr. Montgomery said the woman was still believed to be alive, at age 107.

As I glanced around the room, I saw to my left different types of Haley memorabilia for sale, including copies of his book *Roots*. To my right was a picture with all the cast members from the two miniseries. Some had passed, but many were still alive, like LeVar Burton, who played Kunta, and Maya Angelou, who played his grandmother. As I looked at the picture, I thought about some of the scenes from *Roots: The Next Generations*. I remember marveling at the pride and courage of a young Kunta, who refused to answer to the slave name Toby as he dangled from his wrists and was whipped to near unconsciousness. But I was touched even more by the old black man called Fiddler, played by Louis Gossett Jr., who cradled Kunta in his arms after his limp body was cut down and gently patted his face with water.

"What you care what that white man say," said a teary-eyed

Fiddler. "You know who you be. Kunta. That's who you always be. There go' be another day."

I was twenty-four when the show aired and had just chosen journalism as my profession. I was so moved by the scene that I used it as the topic of a column. The care shown by Fiddler for Kunta symbolized to me the kind of relationship fathers should have with their sons, grandfathers with their grandsons, older men in general with any young boy who's being whipped by life's tribulations. It displayed the kind of encouragement that says: "Stay the course, no matter how tough times get. I've been there, and everything is going to be all right."

Another memorable scene was when Haley, played by James Earl Jones, discovers an old *griot*—oral historian—in Gambia. "You old African! I found you . . . I found you!" he exclaimed with tears welling up in his eyes.

I took one last look at the picture of the cast, then back up at the old African woman, before resting my eyes once again on the picture of Haley looking off into the distance. Suddenly, an eerie chill went down my spine. I had a feeling there was a bigger story here than just the museum.

As I followed Mr. Montgomery's tour of the house, it was like listening to a tape recorder. As old as he was, he never missed a beat. It was as if someone were whispering in his ear. When we got to the living room, I realized a shocking parallel. On the mantel was a picture of a griot and a young man standing a few steps behind his left shoulder. Mr. Montgomery said the griot was the one who told Haley about his ancestors— the old African he'd found in Gambia. Even today, Africans believe that when a griot dies, it's as if a library has burned to the ground. The griots symbolize how all human ancestry goes back to some place and time when there was no writing.

"In the past," Mr. Montgomery said, "this house was visited by leaders from nineteen African countries. One of the leaders was from the Mandinka tribe and identified the old man in the picture as a Mandinka. He tells me this man has nearly five hundred years of tribal history in his head, and this boy never says anything but follows him around listening to his stories. When he dies, the boy must take over."

Mr. Montgomery sometimes traveled with Haley and listened to the stories Haley told about his encounters. But not just that; because they were about the same age, Mr. Montgomery was able to give his own perspective about the times in which they both grew up. As I listened to him, I realized my position in the room. I was just a few steps behind him.

I became more and more engrossed with what this curator was saying as the tour continued. He talked about when he was little, he and the other children wanted to go to school but often couldn't, because they had to pick cotton in the hot sun, many times all day. So when they did go to school, they tried to learn as much as possible. He told me that one time when he was having trouble with his lesson, his mother had told him to pray to God, and that the Creator would help him. He did what she said, and after a few months, he was the smartest student in the class.

I thought about the importance of today's youngsters hearing his story, especially those who don't want to go to school.

But it wasn't just education. There were so many things he said during the tour that could better the lives of others. His words of wisdom were like a mental dose of medicine for the painful and uncertain times in which we now lived.

After the tour, I knew what the lead of my story would be. But I couldn't stop thinking about Mr. Montgomery. I kept saying to myself, *You've got to tell others about him.* He was a jewel, rich in history and wisdom, tucked away in a rural West Tennessee town. I felt as if I had discovered a treasure. And for a little while I sensed the jubilation Haley must have felt when he found the oral historian who unlocked the door to his past. Like him, I couldn't wait to tell the world what I'd found.

I decided to drive to Memphis to see my family before heading home to Nashville. I told some of my family members about my trip, and the very next day we all went to Henning. They were all moved as I had been; some of them even became emotional.

Mr. Montgomery and I stayed in touch. On one of my family visits, I stopped by just to say hello. He was done for the day and said he was glad I'd come by, because he had something to talk to me about. It was then that he told me Haley had planned to write a book about him but died before doing so. He even pulled out a safe and showed me the audiotapes of Haley's interviews with him. I listened to a couple of them, and I felt an eeriness as I heard Haley's voice.

Mr. Montgomery said writers visiting the museum from as far away as Germany and Canada had inquired about writing a book about him, without even knowing Haley had planned to write one. But he said they were pushy, and he didn't feel comfortable with any of them. However, he said there was something about me that made him think about the book. He also said I was "young and sort of unassuming," and he liked that. After much prayer, he'd come to the conclusion that he wanted *me* to write about his life and finish what Haley started. I was greatly honored, of course, but I didn't know if it was a task I could undertake. I'd never written a book before. Would I be able to do him justice? Would I be able to tell his story in such a way that people would find him as fascinating as I did? I told Mr. Montgomery I'd think about it.

As I was leaving, I looked once again at the picture of Haley looking off into the distance. For some reason, Haley wanted to revisit the dock in Annapolis, Maryland, after his completion of *Roots*. Maybe it wasn't just a vast ocean or visions of slave ships he saw. Maybe he was looking for something.

I contemplated Mr. Montgomery's request for about three weeks, then called him back and told him I would do it. This is his story—a story about a twentieth-century slave who rose to the rank of mayor.

CHAPTER 1

TWENTIETH-CENTURY SLAVES

Where justice is denied, where poverty is enforced,
where ignorance prevails, and where any one class
is made to feel that society is in an organized
conspiracy to oppress, rob, and degrade them,
neither persons nor property will be safe.
—FREDERICK DOUGLASS

F red Montgomery was born in Lauderdale County,
Tennessee, on November 22, 1916. Back then, cotton was
the resource that fueled the county's economy. It furnished the
capital that built houses, sent children to school, paid bills,
underwrote businesses, and tied black families to the earth as

sharecroppers. Black men, women, and children planted, then tilled, and finally harvested each year's crop to share on supposed "halves" with landowners, whom many sharecroppers often called boss man. The sharecroppers always owed the boss man money for rent, food, and loans on last year's harvest. With the law in their pockets, landowners kept sharecroppers working on the lands until the debts were paid. Basically, sharecroppers were no more than twentieth-century slaves. Fred and his family were among them.

His father, also named Fred Montgomery, whom he called Papa, was a neatly dressed, reddish-colored man who stood close to six feet tall. Papa didn't say much, and he didn't express himself well. But even though he didn't say it, his family knew he loved them. He worked hard, spending all his time trying to make some kind of a living. The best he could manage was to sharecrop and barber on the side.

Papa's wife, Ionie, Fred's mama, was a petite woman who stood no more than five feet tall and weighed less than a hundred pounds. But her spirit and hot temper made her appear seven feet tall. Nobody messed with Mama.

When Fred was born, Papa sharecropped on Mr. Bob Lewis's farm and made about $150 a year. That wasn't a lot even back then. So sometimes on weekends, if he didn't go to the field, he worked at the barbershop in Henning, giving haircuts and shaves for thirty-five cents.

Fred was the seventh of thirteen children, and he and his family lived on the Lewis farm for about five years. As young as he was, Fred was determined to do something to help his family make ends meet. At five, he was thought to be too young to endure the laborious task of picking cotton in the extreme heat from early in the morning to late in the evening. He realized this when, on the first day he went to the field, he didn't get a sack to pick like the older folks. His mama said he was too small and couldn't pick enough. Well, Fred set out to prove her wrong. He got a bucket and started picking. Each time it got full, he emptied it into a large basket. This got the attention of Mr. Lewis, who decided to weigh the basket when he saw it was nearly full.

"Well, I'll be dogged. You lacking three pounds of having a hundred," he said. "I tell you what you do. You go back out there and pick as hard as you can, so you can have a hundred."

A good picking was about two hundred pounds, so Fred considered one hundred admirable. Running back out in the field, energized by Mr. Lewis's challenge, Fred picked as fast as his little hands would let him. By this time they were bloody from cuts caused by the sharp edges between the hulls, a common misfortune cotton pickers came to accept. But that didn't slow him. When he thought he'd reached his mark, he ran back over to Mr. Lewis. His mother had walked over after noticing the spectacle.

"Ionie," Mr. Lewis called.

"Yes, sir," she replied.

"This boy go' be a goodin. He done picked one hundred pounds. Come here, boy, and get this nickel."

Now that was quite a bit of money for a five-year-old. Lye soap couldn't have washed the grin off Fred's face. Ionie also smiled, reluctantly. It wasn't the future she wanted for her children, but her little boy's determination let her know that he wouldn't be afraid to face life's challenges in the future. He would be a survivor, as would his siblings. And Ionie was determined to do her part to help them succeed. Even though she didn't have any schooling, she was full of wisdom. One day she called all her children to her and gave each one a wooden match. She then told the youngest to try to break it. He did. Then she took out about ten of the matches, put them together, and tied a string around them. She told the oldest to try to break it. When he couldn't, she said to all of them in a sweet, motherly voice: "Together we stand. Divided we fall."

It was this belief, and their trust in God, that sustained most black families, especially under the tough conditions in which they lived. The children often got colds from water leaking through the roof and wetting the bedcovers when it rained. Snowflakes slipped through the walls in the winter. Ionie did her best to provide warmth by piling quilts and cotton sacks over the children. She would move from one child to the next, asking if they had colds or fevers. If they were congested, on the spot, Ionie became Dr. Mama, and with her mouth she sucked the cold from their noses so they could breathe.

Sometimes she would put tar on a rag and pin it around their chests, as well as green leaves from a peach tree. It was an old healing remedy that had been passed down through generations. Supposedly, as the rag and leaves dried, they took away the fever. Finally, she would kneel at their bedsides and pray, often fighting tears. All the children lay still while she prayed, none of them daring to make a move or a sound that might interrupt her search for God. Her crying let them know she had made contact, and they would be well soon.

Her faith was a balm for their troubles.

CHAPTER 2

KEEPING THE FAITH

Truly I tell you, if you have faith as small as a
mustard seed, you can say to this mountain,
"Move from here to there," and it will move.
Nothing will be impossible for you.
—MATTHEW 17:20

As Fred grew older, he began to ponder this concept of
kneeling, closing one's eyes, and thanking this person called God for meager things. *Who was he anyway?* he
thought. Until he was old enough to know for himself, he
decided he would just mimic Mama, Papa, and other people,
who in their distress called to God or another name he often
heard: Jesus Christ. Whoever this fellow was, he was like

a member of the family when they were sick or in need of something. Fred kept thinking one day he'd meet him. So, in case he did, he thought the best way to prepare for that day would be to practice acting like the person he believed was God's best man: the minister.

Standing on a tree stump in 1922, Fred, who was now six, would gather children from the neighborhood around him and proceed to give a so-called fire-and-brimstone sermon, often recalling stories his mama read to him from the Bible. If a chicken or dog had died, Fred felt it was his duty to give a funeral.

"We are here today to pay farewell to this dog, who will be missed by us all," Fred would say in a crescendo voice over the shoebox used as a coffin. "He was a good dog. So he's headed to heaven."

Bad dogs were thought to be hell-bound, of course. But Minister Fred prayed for their poor souls anyway. And he expected his congregation to do the same. He was a feisty pastor. If his members didn't shout as he wanted them to, then Fred felt they'd backslid, and he told them they needed to return later to "confess hope in Christ again."

His actions may have seemed comical to some, but Fred was actually developing an early relationship with God—a relationship that unbeknownst to him would grow stronger as he got older. As a child it helped console him and his siblings, especially during tough times when they didn't know where their next meal would come from. On one such occasion, he heard Papa and Mama whispering.

"Fred, I ain't complaining, but there's nothing in the house to eat 'cept grease and flour," Ionie said. There was no criticism in her voice, but there was concern.

"Don't worry," Papa said. "I'm going out now and kill us a rabbit or two."

His voice lacked passion, but Ionie knew he meant well, so she just sighed and smiled.

Papa was a great hunter, a great provider. He was like an African warrior who set out to get food for the tribe, knowing that nourishment of many depended on his day's catch. Fred and his brothers and sisters went to the fields that day and picked cotton till it was nearly dark. Their bellies churned and their mouths watered as they thought about eating a rabbit. Off in the distance, they saw Papa returning with his catch but couldn't quite make out what it was. They were so hungry and expectant they stopped picking cotton and began walking toward their little shack, picking up broken limbs as they went to build up the fire they knew Mama had probably already started. They beat Papa to the house, and Mama, as expected, had started the fire. When Papa came inside, he pulled out the meal for the evening: a quail. Disappointment filled their faces.

"Is that all you got?" Ionie asked, trying not to sound too let down.

"This is it," Papa replied.

He had a tone they'd never heard before. There was shame in his voice as he handed his wife the small bird. Ionie didn't say anything else. She knew he was just as disappointed as they all were, and that he had done his best to kill a rabbit or something bigger than the quail.

Like a battlefield cook working quickly and efficiently to feed hungry troops, Ionie snatched the feathers off that bird, gutted it, and chopped it into small pieces. Regardless of its size, that quail was going to be supper for fifteen people. She then took a skillet, greased it, and put it on top of the stove, which was now well heated. She poured flour and water into the skillet to make gravy, then added the little pieces of quail. Inside the stove was some corn bread that was almost ready. The aroma from it was so sweet and thick that if the children could have cut air, they would have had an appetizer.

When the bread was finally done, Ionie rationed out the pieces of meat between herself and Papa. Then she told the children to sit on the floor and she handed them their tin tops, which they used as plates. Each of them got one piece of meat. The rest was gravy with large chunks of corn bread. Before they ate, as always, Papa told all of them to bow their heads and say a prayer of thanks. For some strange reason, no matter how little they had to eat, every time they prayed, their bellies were as tight as though they had just eaten a feast. They never went hungry.

Whether it was sitting at the dinner table, kneeling by the side of the bed, or singing in the fields, black families turned to God for strength and comfort. Songs like "Swing Low, Sweet Chariot" and "Soon I Will Be Done" gave them some serenity as they sharecropped, bent over for hours under the sweltering heat of a sun that seemed to have no mercy.

The work was backbreaking and degrading. But they were a special people who sought a special strength. With no land, little income, and scarcity in other resources, they displayed a faith that seemed to have no measure. They continued to look upward, sending their prayers and melodies to a Creator they truly believed would hear and empower them against their greatest foe: racism.

• • •

Fred often talked about his faith in God. He told me about his childhood experiences when God answered his prayer. "I know God will answer a child's prayer," said Fred. "He answered mine."

When I think about my own childhood, I realized that I, too, was introduced to God at an early age. My mother, like Ionie, would always make sure I said my prayers before going to bed. And when I visited Daddy Roy and my grandmother, they always thanked God for the food and other provisions. But it was my grandmother's relationship with God, in partic-ular, that intrigued me the most. When she talked about him, I didn't envision a deity somewhere faraway, but a best friend with whom she conversed every day and who comforted her when in need. As Fred grew older, he also saw God as a close friend.

"I never make any kind of decision without first praying about it," Fred once said. "If when I wake up in the morning and I have a good feeling, then I know that's a yes from God.

If I feel uncomfortable or uneasy, then that's a no. I trust him wholeheartedly."

When I visited my maternal grandparents' church, where my mother's sisters also attended, I noticed similar spiritual relationships. No matter how tough their week had been, they seemed to find peace of mind in the words of songs they sang praising God. Oftentimes they would stand with their eyes tightly closed and sway back and forth with their hands raised. Every now and then, tears would seep through their eyelids and run down their cheeks, not out of sorrow, but rather out of joyful release. At age nine, I wanted the same relationship with God that they had. I wanted to know this Friend.

One day, my parents and I drove to the country to visit my grandparents. I had a pony there, and I was looking forward to riding him. However, it had started to rain, and my father said if it continued, I wouldn't be able to ride. I was disappointed because it had been almost a month since our last visit. I wanted it to stop raining. But as I looked at the darkened skies that stretched as far as I could see, my chances of riding seemed slim. Then I remembered something one of my aunts once told me.

"If you want something, ask God for it," she said. "But in asking, you've got to believe that he will answer. You've got to have faith."

I closed my eyes. And in a silent prayer, I asked God for the rain to go away and for the clouds to clear. Suddenly, the rain stopped. And about a minute later, I was amazed at what started to happen. The dark clouds began to disperse, and as far as I could see was a beautiful blue sky. It didn't rain anymore that day, and I was able to ride my pony.

Some skeptics might think what happened that day was merely a coincidence. But I don't think so. I believe a little boy simply called on God, and he answered a child's prayer.

CHAPTER 3

A DIFFERENT COLOR

There is an incredible amount of magic and
feistiness in black men that nobody has been
able to wipe out. But everybody has tried.
—TONI MORRISON

I t wasn't something she enjoyed doing. But when it came to
dealing with white folks, Fred's mother, Ionie, made sure
her children minded their manners. "If you're walking in the
street and a white person is coming your way, then you get off
the street," she would tell them.

They were also told to use back doors and bathrooms and
water fountains labeled "Colored." Black mothers and fathers
attempted to instill in their children the laws of the times to
keep them from being confronted by whites looking to make

trouble. But many times, confrontation was inevitable. Such was the case with a black businessman named Will Palmer.

Will was the wealthiest black man in Henning. He was an inspiration to the blacks, but most of the whites envied him because he had more money than some of them put together. As a young man, Will worked at a lumber company for fifty cents a day. The owner of the company was a heavy drinker and mismanaged a lot of his money. He got so far behind in his payments that he ended up losing the business. If it hadn't been for Will's hard work in trying to meet the customers' needs, the business probably would have been shut down long before.

Later, ten white businessmen realized a lumber company was very much needed in the area, so they cosigned a loan and bailed the company out. They decided to put Will in charge of the business since he practically ran it anyway. Over the next ten years, Will prospered, making enough money to pay off the debt and own the business himself. Then, in 1921, he built his own home. All this was definitely a bitter pill for some whites to swallow. They began to harass Will and his family with cross-burnings and death threats. Older blacks believed every time a cross was burned, someone was going to die. Ionie could see Will's house sitting up on the hill from her window. She often stayed up late at night peeking through her curtain and praying that no harm would come to them. Her prayers were soon answered.

One day, two Ku Klux Klansmen rode up to the house and called for Will to come out. Will, who never really showed fear, did so. "You better not close your eyes in that house," one of them said. "It's too good a house for a nigger. And if you move in it, we go' burn it down on you and your family."

About that time, the grandson of Dr. D. M. Henning, after whom the town was named, happened to be passing by. He told the Klansmen to leave Will and his family alone. They were, of course, reluctant. But they knew Mr. Henning was a powerful man, and so they did as he said. Area blacks rejoiced that such a prestigious white man had spoken up for Will and his family. During the following week, each night as the sun set, a group of about seven to ten black women held hands and formed a circle in Will's front yard as they prayed and sang hymns.

"God always got somebody to take care of the poor and the righteous," they joyously testified.

The actions of the businessmen and Mr. Henning showed that there were some whites who believed in fairness. But many others shared the mentality of the Klansmen, threatening blacks and perpetuating demeaning behavior. Some whites demanded that black men and women call white boys over the age of thirteen "sir." As young as he was, Fred knew this wasn't right. He didn't have to act a certain way with other black boys, so what was different about the boys a shade or two lighter than him? Nevertheless, he did his best to mind the words of his mother and other elders.

On nice days, Fred and his grandmother would fish together. She told him about her grandparents, who were born slaves and auctioned off like cattle. Though beaten and stripped from their loved ones, she said they trusted in God to see them through the terrible times they faced. She encouraged her little grandson to do the same, despite the racism that glared at him each day. "I don't know why things happen the way they do," she told him. "But God's going to make it right. There's going to be a better day." Fred tried to be optimistic. But, one day, the glaring got the best of him.

Back then there was a gang of white boys who rode their ponies right through his and his friends' marble games. The ponies' hooves would kick dust up in their faces and grind the marbles deep into the ground. This particular day, Fred had had enough. When the boys flew by, something in him snapped. He jumped to his feet, snatched up the first rock he saw, and threw it, hitting one of the boys in the back of the head. The boy screamed, and they all turned to chase Fred and his friends, who had taken off in different directions. Fred ran as fast as he could all the way home and into the kitchen.

"Why you runnin', boy?" his mama asked.

"Just runnin'," he answered, not daring to look her in the eye.

He went to his room and sat there feeling vindicated. But as he thought about what he'd done, he suddenly felt a sense of sadness. *I could've hurt that boy bad*, he realized. *Why'd I do that? I've got arms and legs and eyes just like him. The only difference is our skin.*

Fred never told his mama what had happened that day. He never forgot it either. The guilt and anger stayed inside him.

• • •

Racism is a sickness that shouldn't be inflicted on anyone. But it's truly sad when children are exposed to it. Fred's introduction to racism as a child reminded me of my own childhood. And like him, I, too, thought white people were just plain bad.

The idea struck me in the head—literally—in the third grade, when a white boy hit me in the face with a lunch box and blackened my right eye. I wanted to believe he was just having a bad day, but I later learned that he just didn't like black people. A mentality he got from his parents.

My opinion of whites was drawn from older blacks, who would often comment, "You just can't trust them." They were the ones who had been called nigger, pushed to the back of the bus, and spit on during lunch-counter sit-ins and other protests in their attempt to gain equal rights.

Dr. Harold Taylor, an oral surgeon, was one of those pioneers. He was among a group of people who gathered at a college in Memphis, walked next door to a predominantly white Presbyterian church, and tried to enter. When the elders and deacons refused to let them in, they knelt in prayer outside the church. Other times they marched and did sit-ins in downtown, where they would be cussed at and spat on, a degradation considered worse than being hit. Yet, they were trained to be nonviolent and not to fight back. I admire their passiveness, because I don't think I could have been as resistant. I probably would have ended up in jail for the rest of my life or dead—which just may have been my fate if I'd acted as I felt one day in the summer of 1994.

It was close to noon, but I was in the mood for breakfast food. Most places near my home had started serving lunch, so I decided to stop at a twenty-four-hour restaurant I knew would have what I wanted. It was a chain that had recently come under fire for discrimination on the part of some of its white employees. But I figured not all the restaurants had such problems. I guess you could say I wanted to give them the benefit of the doubt.

I should have known something was wrong when I walked in. The white customer before me was greeted cheerfully, but there were only silence and stares when I entered. After I sat down, I noticed the two waitresses standing and talking with the cook. They had glanced my way when I was seated but continued to ignore me. After close to thirty minutes, a customer interrupted them and nodded in my direction. With a look of reluctance, one of the waitresses came over and asked me if I was ready to order in a hurried tone as if she had somewhere to be. I was irate. I wanted to tell her to take a flying leap. Instead, I bit my tongue and told her politely, "No thanks. I think I'll go somewhere else." There was silence and stunned faces as I left.

I tried not to be naive. But it was hard for me to believe that, even decades after the sit-ins, I was still not considered equal enough to be served like everybody else.

Like Fred Montgomery, after having his game of marbles disrupted, the anger stayed with me.

CHAPTER 4

EDUCATION

If you are planning for a year, sow rice;
if you are planning for a decade, plant trees;
if you are planning for a lifetime, educate people.
—**CHINESE PROVERB**

When Fred was growing up, education was seen as one of the main ways to beat racism. During slavery, some people risked life and limb to learn to read and write. After the Civil War, emancipation, like a mighty river, swept through the South, washing away the chains and shackles. Even though they faced ridicule, the newly freed people insisted on book learning. They flocked to hastily established schools founded by churches of almost every denomination.

Fred started school at age six. He and his seven siblings attended at the same time. Mama and Papa couldn't afford to give them all pencils, so they bought four and broke them in half. But the children didn't care as long as they got a chance to go to school. As young as they were, they knew that school was their main way out of poverty, which they shook hands with daily. Since school lasted only four to six months out of the year, they were always disappointed when the landowner wanted them to work his fields instead. Such occurrences were painful for Fred.

One morning, when he had on his best clothes to head to school, Papa came in with a solemn look on his face. Fred knew some bad news was coming. "Put on your work clothes, son," Papa said. "He needs some extra help today."

Papa knew Fred was hurt, but he didn't say anything. He just left the room. Fred did what he said, but before going to the fields, he went to his mama. With tears in his eyes, he begged her to ask Papa to let him go to school the next day. Ionie gently rubbed his face, then put her arms around him and hugged him tight. It was all she could do. As long as they lived on another man's land and worked his fields, neither she nor Papa had any control over their schooling. It was a situation many sharecroppers faced.

One teacher, Mrs. Carrie Turner, vowed to change that. "My mission here is to rob the cotton fields of cotton hands," she said. She was unique in that she was a black woman married to a white man, Jim Turner. That allowed her to make such statements without public censure. She loved her people and was determined to do whatever she could to see them progress. Ms. Lizzette Murray was no different. A tall, tough black woman, Ms. Murray wore a tight corset that made her walk as straight as a board. She stood in front of her students like an army general, and she was as strict as one too. The fresh-cut switch was always there to remind them of that. Stern as she was, she also loved them, and they loved her.

In that little one-room schoolhouse, they felt valued. They felt they could be somebody. Fred and the other children were taught to respect their teachers. They were told their teachers were the only ones qualified to keep them from being ignorant. Fred and his older sister Evergene promised to respect their teachers and to learn as much as their minds could absorb. They fantasized about the jobs they'd get with an education, and what they'd do with the money. Evergene, who was the second oldest, said she planned to buy a fancy hat with a ribbon hanging down the back and bows for her dresses and slippers. Then she pranced around sassily in front of Fred, demonstrating how she would show off her new accessories. Fred, on the other hand, just wanted some pants of his own. He'd been wearing his brothers' hand-me-downs, and by the time he got them, there were usually two holes in the knees and two in the butt. He believed all that would change after Ms. Murray's schooling. "I'm gonna get a job and make some money," Fred said. "Then I'm go' buy me two brand-new pair of breeches my brothers ain't never had on."

Fred's family moved to Henning in the summer of 1925. They lived only a block from the school, so sometimes his mama would walk him. One day, they passed a somewhat large, bluish-colored house with four white columns in the front. Fred thought white people lived there. But then he saw a little black boy playing with a ball in the yard. *Could he be the housekeeper's son?* he thought. The little boy saw Fred staring and asked if he wanted to play. They tossed the ball a couple of times before Mama told him to come on or he'd be late for school. The little boy asked them to wait a minute, then ran into the house. When he came back out, a woman just a little bit bigger than Mama was with him.

"Hello, my name is Cynthia," she said. "My grandson Alex wants to know if he can walk to school with you this morning."

Mama said that would be fine, and they all walked down the road together. Alex and Fred hung out at school and became good friends. As it turned out, Ms. Murray was Alex's aunt and his grandfather was Will Palmer. Alex came to live with his grandparents after his mother, Bertha, died, and his father, Simon Haley, was unable to raise him by himself. Alex went to live with his father after he remarried some years later.

After school, Alex and Fred would often go hunting for hickory nuts or skinny-dipping, depending on the time of the year. Because he was three years older than Alex, Fred became sort of a big brother to him. And like most big brothers, he got Alex in trouble quite frequently. Grandma Cynthia kept a tight rein on Alex. But one day, while she was picking some greens at her sister's house, Fred persuaded Alex to sneak away so they could go skinny-dipping. Fred, who was about eleven at the time, met Alex behind his grandma's house, then they took off through a cornfield and across a bridge to a nearby creek. Now, Alex had never been in the water before, so he was hesitant. Fred saw that he was nervous and decided to take off his clothes and jump in to show him it was okay. "Come on, little buddy, it's all right," said Fred, wading in the water. "I'm not going to let anything happen to you."

Alex had taken off his clothes, but he still refused to jump. Fred then splashed water up on the bank to try to get him wet. Alex finally stepped forward but then slipped, falling into the water like a bear cub learning to swim for the first time. He splashed around and spit water for a few seconds before Fred swam over to him. He calmed down once he realized the water wasn't that deep. Then a big smile came across his face when he noticed he was actually floating.

"See, I told you I wasn't going to let anything happen to you," Fred said.

But Alex didn't need protection in the water; it was when he got out. As they walked soaking wet down the road leading to Alex's house, waiting on the porch with her hands on her hips and a stare sharper than a butcher knife was Grandma Cynthia. "Alexander Palmer Haley," she yelled. "You get up here right now!"

When she called him by his whole name, he knew he was in trouble. Fred and the other boys with them knew it also, which is why they scattered like rabbits when they heard it. Alex's grandmother didn't whip him that day. She waited until she saw him and Fred after church the next Sunday, and then she let them both have it. When she finished telling them how disappointed she was and how they had broken her trust, they were ashamed to even look at her. Alex later turned to Fred and said, "I kind of wish she had whipped us."

When they weren't skinny-dipping or getting into other mischief, Fred and Alex spent a lot of time writing love letters to little girls, even though they didn't know what in the world they were talking about. They borrowed verses from poetry books that Alex had at his house. The letters would start out, "How are you today? Fine, I hope." Then it would continue, "As sure as the vine grows around the stump, you're my darlin' sugar lump," or "The river's wide and I can't step it, I love you baby and I just can't help it." Fred noticed that Alex was better at writing the letters, even though he was younger. The girls seemed to think so also.

Alex's folks had money, so he didn't have to worry about sharecropping. But Fred still had to miss many days to help Papa in the field. His family had moved off Mr. Lewis's land, but they still sharecropped for him. Eventually, Fred missed too many days, causing him to fail the third grade. Ms. Murray thought he was goofing off and gave him whippings when he continued to do poorly, but he just didn't have time to study. By the time he'd finished in the fields, he was too tired to do anything but sleep.

Back then, when you got a whipping at school, you got one at home too. One day, when Fred got home and told his mama the trouble he was having with his lesson, she didn't whip him but rather gave him some advice. She pulled him close to her, kissed his forehead, and said, "God will help you get your lesson." She told him to take his book and put it under his pillow each night before going to bed, then pray to God for help. "When you get up the next morning," she said, "the lesson will be in your head." Mama had never been wrong before, so he did what she said. He knew she and God had a pretty good relationship, because whenever she called on him when Fred was sick, he got better. Fred gave it a try, hopping out of bed in the middle of the night and praying in his cold room. "God, please help me get my lesson," he prayed earnestly.

One night, his papa caught him and asked what he was doing. He answered that he was asking God to help him better understand his schoolwork. In his usual quiet manner, Papa just turned and left.

Fred kept sending up prayers for a while, never giving up hope that he'd make some type of connection with God, as Mama always seemed to. Then it happened. After about two weeks, his lessons seemed to get easier, and he started remembering things when called upon at school. After two months, he had caught up with everybody else, and Ms. Murray told him he was ready to move up to the fourth grade.

Before graduation, students had to recite a special poem: "If a task is once begun / Never leave it until it's done / Be the labor great or small / Do it well or not at all." Ms. Murray wrote the poem on the board and gave each student two weeks to memorize it. Of course, it didn't take Fred that long. He was now personally acquainted with the Person his mother had called upon those nights beside his bed. He learned the poem in a day.

• • •

Fred's story reminded me of the importance of education and the invaluableness of teachers, since it is education that opens doors.

"We were told," he said, "that the teacher was the only one qualified to lead us from ignorance and keep us from being raggedy and poor. We respected them."

When I look back, Hattie Caldwell and Erma Branch, my first-and second-grade teachers, had a lot to do with my success today. I must admit, I didn't care too much for school at first. It was like greens and spinach—the things I was told I should eat to stay healthy but didn't want to. My mother drilled into my head that if I wanted to be somebody one day, I needed an education. Ms. Caldwell reinforced that idea in school. Unlike Fred's Ms. Lizzette Murray, she didn't discipline us with a switch. But Ms. Caldwell didn't need to be physical. At nearly five feet seven, she had a look and a voice that let us know she meant business. However, I'm sure there were times she would have liked to snatch me up.

I had this thing about hiding my bad grades. Whenever I got one, I would either trash the assignment or stick it in the back of my folder. I didn't realize it, but Ms. Caldwell saw me throw away some of the assignments. She didn't say anything because she wanted to see how long I'd keep it up. One day, when my dad came to pick me up from school, Ms. Caldwell told him what I'd been doing. He then told my mother when I got home. Needless to say, my mother gave me a severe tongue-lashing. After that, she made sure she saw all my grades. If there was something I didn't understand, she took the time to help me. And if I was confused about something, she told me to ask Ms. Caldwell, to whom she had given full martial law rights. They were like the tight defense of a football team. If I ran something past Ms. Caldwell, my mother was there to tackle me.

By the time they were finished with me, I was ready for Ms. Branch. A slender woman with a mellow voice, Ms. Branch wasn't as stern as Ms. Caldwell, but her attentiveness was the same or better. She took time to make sure each of her students understood their lesson. And she taught us early on about great black leaders, such as Sojourner Truth, Madam C. J. Walker, George Washington Carver, and W. E. B. DuBois, just to name a few. She showed us films about different parts of the world that took us beyond our troubled neighborhoods and allowed us to dream, just as Ms. Murray and Mrs. Carrie Turner lifted Fred and other students above the cotton fields.

I never saw Ms. Caldwell or Ms. Branch again. However, my mother informed me some years later that Ms. Branch had died of cancer. My hometown newspaper had done an article about her. It said that even as the cancer ate away at her body, she continued to go to work. She made sure all her grades were in order and other little details were handled up until her last day. She was dedicated. It's because of these two black women that I now have great respect for all teachers. In addition to their own families, they had an extended family of hundreds of students they cared for as if they were their own. And that's saying a lot, considering the meager salaries some teachers make, and the fact that they're cussed at and even threatened by students who don't appreciate what they're trying to do.

It's a long way from the days when youngsters cried to go to school and included their teachers in their prayers. But, like Fred, I never forgot those who helped lead me out of ignorance.

"God bless Mama and Papa," Fred would pray as a little boy before going to bed.

His mother, praying next to him, would then ask, "What next, boy?"

And Fred would reply, "God bless my teacher."

That goes double for me.

CHAPTER 5

THAT SKINNY-LEG GIRL

The meeting of two personalities is like the
contact of two chemical substances: if there
is any reaction, both are transformed.
—CARL JUNG

As he got older, Fred continued to do well in school. He
excelled in academics as well as athletics and drama. He was
the captain of the boys' basketball team and played the lead
role in several plays. He was the darling young gentleman of
the community, and nearly every black mother with a daughter
of courting age wanted him to meet their daughters. And at
age sixteen, his interest for the opposite sex had kicked into
high gear. He was long past letter writing, and with his little
buddy Alex gone to live with his father and stepmother in

Arkansas, he was left alone to explore one of God's sweetest gifts to man.

There were several young women Fred had his eyes on, but Ernestine Bond, a chocolate, skinny-leg girl, was the one who occupied his mind. He actually saw her for the first time when he was six and she was five, but he didn't pay her any attention because he didn't like girls then. She'd wanted to play with the little toy rifle he had with him, but he refused to let her touch it.

Fred didn't see her much after that. But one spring evening, when he was about sixteen, he saw her standing next to a tree at a church outing. Her neatly fitting skirt-and-blouse outfit, freshly hot-combed hair, and plum-colored lips got his attention. He told her how nice he thought she looked. She blushed, said thank you, and smiled. Fred was hooked. After talking for a while, his stomach began to feel funny, as if, as they say, butterflies were in it. He pushed on.

"By the way," he began, feigning confidence, "may I walk you home from school sometimes?"

"Oh, I don't know," she said, "I'll have to ask my mother."

Butterflies were winging their way through his stomach again. *Was she just saying that or did she really intend to do it?* he wondered.

Later that week Fred walked her home, and so began their relationship. Most of their times together were fun. There were a lot of things they had in common and some things they didn't. Dancing was one of them.

One night at a party, Ernestine was on the floor dancing up

a storm. Fred couldn't dance, so he just stood and watched with increasing jealousy as she twisted and turned with another fellow. Having had just about enough, he strutted past Ernestine, went up to Trout Bates, a girl he had known before Ernestine, and planted a big kiss on her lips. About a minute later he felt a hand twirl him around and *pow*, down he went. When he got up and regained his senses, the left side of his face felt as if it had been hit with a brick. He thought it might have been some guy who liked Trout that had popped him. But it turned out to be Ernestine. Boy, was she mad. Embarrassed, he went outside to escape the laughter and taunts from his friends. After some time had passed, he and Ernestine eventually made up.

Fred and Ernestine had mainly just kissed. But like most teenage boys, Fred became curious and tried to see if he could get Ernestine to do more, to go all the way. She refused. However, one day, out of nowhere, she said she would. But only if Fred promised to marry her if he got her pregnant. With his hormones raging, he agreed. They kept it up for about two years. Then it happened.

Ernestine didn't show up for school, and she sent a note through her sister, Martha, telling Fred that she was pregnant. At that moment, it seemed as if the whole world had dropped out from under him. His teachers and the people in the community had always said he was going to make something of himself. What would they say now? Fred, a father? He was still a boy himself. He thought about doing as others had done and leave town and pretend it never happened. But he didn't want to put Ernestine through that kind of embarrassment by abandoning her. He loved her. So he decided to drop out of school and marry her, if she would have him.

When the news got to his mama, she wasn't happy at all, and neither was Papa. They wanted Fred to get an education, to break the cycle, to be different. But this was an old, tired story for them, and they told him what he needed to do. "You having any schooling is no better than that girl," his mama said. That was her way of telling him that providing for Ernestine and his child—his family—was more important than school. It was a sad truth.

In 1935, barely nineteen, Fred had to become a man. The road to manhood was already getting bumpy and financially tough, and he wasn't even married yet. They didn't have the $3 to pay for a marriage license and the $2 for a preacher. Fortunately, Fred had $3 coming from his janitor's job, and his oldest sister, Sally, gave him $2.26. But Mr. Light Stokely charged $1 to drive them to Ripley to get the license. Ernestine's mama, Mrs. Lela, saved the day. She gave them a silver dollar to pay Mr. Stokely and directed them to a cousin who was a jackleg preacher. She said he'd probably marry them for free. After they got the license and Mrs. Lela signed it (they were too young), they went looking for the preacher.

They found him plowing near his house. When he saw them approach, along with Mrs. Lela, who was there as a witness, he unhitched his mule and motioned for them to follow him. Once inside his home, he took out his hymnal and began to sing. Then, in a solemn voice, he asked Fred and Ernestine to come before him and started praying. When he stopped, he looked down and saw Ernestine grinning. "I'm going to pray some more, young lady," he said sternly. "This is God's work, and God's business is serious business indeed."

"Ernestine," Fred whispered as softly as he could, "if you don't stop grinning, we'll never get married."

The preacher looked up and asked Mrs. Lela if anyone had anything against them getting married. She gave a quick and simple, "No."

After repeating their wedding vows, Fred kissed and hugged Ernestine. He knew they were facing some tough times. Mama and Papa's absence from the wedding was a clear sign of their displeasure. But as he looked into Ernestine's beautiful brown eyes and held her hand, it didn't matter. There was an unexplainable calmness deep in his soul that let him know they'd be all right. If the world were to fall to pieces, he knew they had each other—and a little one on the way. His family.

• • •

I was never really given "the birds and the bees" talk. I mentioned just a few girls to my parents while in high school, so they probably didn't see any need to lecture me at the time. Anyway, the only action I got was an occasional kiss behind the bleachers during a game or a smooch or two outside the dance. For me, French-kissing was like getting to third base. Yeah, I was slow. But I began to gain a little bit of momentum in college. That's when my mother played Dr. Ruth the best way she knew how.

"Now, you behave yourself," she said. "There's nothing wrong with having friends. But you don't need to get all involved with some girl right now. Just concentrate on your lesson. That's what's important."

I listened. At least for a while.

In 1988, the second semester of my freshman year, I met a young lady named Lisa, who had taken an interest in me. She smiled every time I saw her, and some mutual friends told me she had been inquiring about me. I played it off. But one day I saw her on campus and her outfit got my attention. Her snug white sweater and tight-fitting blue jeans accentuated a figure I hadn't noticed before. Suddenly my hormones kicked into another gear, leaving my mind behind. So I approached her. By this time, I had a smile on *my* face. We talked for about an hour, then continued our conversation later that night on the phone. We seemed to be hitting it off.

After about a week, she invited me to her apartment, and I accepted. Looking back, that was probably my mistake number one. After about thirty minutes, we began kissing on her couch. I had graduated to French-kissing, and this sista was prompting me to hit a home run. I didn't have any condoms, but she said that was okay because she was on the pill. I proceeded to bat. Mistake number two.

The same play kept up for the rest of the semester—in my dorm room, her apartment, or her parents' house—until I went home for the summer. One evening, I received a phone call I will never forget. Lisa said she called to see how my summer was going, then dropped a bomb on me.

"I think I'm pregnant," she said.

After taking a few seconds to absorb what she said, I nervously asked, "Are you sure?"

"I'm late," she said, "and I haven't been able to keep anything in my stomach."

"But I thought you were on the pill."

There was silence. Then she replied, "I stopped taking them."

I can't explain how I felt at that moment. It was like being angry and sick at the same time. But what she said next made me feel worse. It was the last thing a wide-eyed, jobless, irresponsible eighteen-year-old wanted to hear.

"If I am, I'm going to keep it," she continued.

I'd never felt so helpless. I knew I wasn't ready to be a father. But if she was pregnant, I had to respect her decision, as Fred had respected Ernestine's. "Ernestine didn't get pregnant by herself," Fred said. "I was just as responsible. And now I had to take responsibility. I could have run away like a lot of young men and left her alone. But I wasn't about to do that. We handled the situation together."

Fred's commitment to taking responsibility was an inspiration to me. I'd like to think I would have done the same. Fortunately, God was merciful in my case. Lisa's pregnancy test came back negative. Apparently, her period was just late that month, and it was a virus that was making her sick.

Needless to say, the incident had a lasting effect on me. Unlike Fred and Ernestine, Lisa and I wouldn't have gotten married. But like Fred, I would have taken responsibility and been in the child's life. However, to avoid any heartache—financial or otherwise—it would have been better if I had waited until marriage to have sex. "It was good advice to wait when I was coming up, and still is," Fred said. "I love Ernestine and my family. But if I was starting over again, I would have waited." He also stressed that being cautious and waiting is the way to avoid getting a sexually transmitted disease, and that it could jeopardize my relationship with the woman I decide to marry.

"How sad, to miss out on a lifetime of love, for temporary pleasure," Fred said. "I was fortunate. You may not be."

CHAPTER 6

FIGHTING THE HATRED

Always forgive your enemies;
nothing annoys them so much.
—OSCAR WILDE

F red and Ernestine spent the early years of their marriage
sharecropping on a farm just outside Henning owned by
Sam Thum. He was one of those white men caught in a time
warp and didn't realize slavery had ended. He was unfair to
Ernestine's parents, as well as the three other families who
worked on his farm. But they didn't have anywhere else to go,
so they had to make do, especially Fred and Ernestine, who
had one child, Charles, and another on the way. Ernestine's
parents insisted they live with them on the farm until they
could get on their feet.

Each family was given a few acres to work, which was just

barely enough to get by. If a family was fortunate enough, they would have enough money to buy food to last them through the winter months. If not, they would have to take on odd jobs to make ends meet. Every two weeks, the boss man would write up what were called orders, a list of things the family needed from the store in town.

If old man Thum approved of what the families put on the list, he would rewrite their items on another list and take it to the store. Fred thought the process was degrading, mainly because he didn't want some old white man knowing what his wife was wearing under her dress. Then there was Thum's abusive attitude. Fred recalled on one occasion a man wanted to get some dried peaches because his mother-in-law was coming to visit and his wife wanted to make some pies. But Thum told him, "Nigger don't need no dried peaches," and scratched it off the list.

Thum would never give money or let the people know exactly how much each item was worth. If he didn't have enough money to pay for everybody's requests, he would borrow from the bank at 7 percent interest. But when it came time for the families to pay him, he would charge 25 percent. The high interest cut the workers' crop profit, which meant a lot of people ended up in debt. And the boss man wanted it that way. He didn't care about the well-being of his workers, just his profit. His treatment of Ernestine's parents was proof of his cold character.

Dusty and Mrs. Lela had been on his farm for more than fifteen years, and they were hard workers. Dusty was a tall, light-skinned man. Mrs. Lela was dark and, judging from her strong frame, looked as though she could have whipped most men in her younger days. But both had gotten old and simply couldn't do what they used to. Dusty was also going blind. The boss man called them deadweight because they weren't producing enough, and he ordered them off his land so a young couple could move into their house.

"I'm go' get me some young niggers to work my farm," Fred overheard him say one day. Ernestine and Fred couldn't believe it. They knew Thum had his ways, but how could he put out some of his most loyal workers? And in winter on top of that? It was like sticking a dagger in their backs. With the help of their son, Ernestine's brother, Dusty and Mrs. Lela managed to find a house in Henning.

In 1937, Fred and Ernestine managed to move to another little vacant house on the farm. From that moment, Fred told Ernestine he was going to start saving to purchase his own house. And he was optimistic. He had dropped out of school, but he was further along than most of the blacks he knew who couldn't even read, let alone spell their own names, like Mrs. Lela. One day he accidentally walked in on Ernestine trying to teach her how to read.

"See, Mama," Ernestine said, writing on a piece of paper, "this is an *L*, an *E*, *L*, and *A* . . . Lela."

Fred fought back tears. What he saw fueled his resolve. He was determined to use the little education he had to get the jobs necessary to get off that farm and build a house. It would be a place for his family as well as Ernestine's parents, so they wouldn't have to ever worry about being put out again. He told Ernestine of his plans, and she began to cry. When he asked what was wrong, she said in a quivering voice, "I just can't see myself owning a house."

Fred took her hand and assured her, "We will. We will."

For years, Fred hustled during the winter months, taking on any kind of job—shoveling coal, unloading trucks, killing rabbits—to save money for a down payment on a house. That meant making sacrifices in order to live off the profit of that year's harvest. One year, he was able to clear twelve dollars picking cotton for Thum, which was more money than he would normally make doing that kind of work. He spent eight dollars on a bed and mattress for the baby, leaving them with only four dollars to stretch from December to March. He told Ernestine to hold on to that money. But Ernestine, being young and slightly stubborn, was determined to do what she wanted.

As Fred was returning from rabbit hunting, he saw a truck leaving the house. Ernestine met him at the door all excited, eager to show him what she had just gotten: some linoleum to put on the floor. It was not something they needed. In a sweet voice, she told him it cost only $3.75. Now, the young couple rarely had major disagreements. But this time, Ernestine had touched a nerve. For a while, Fred was too mad to say anything. Then he took a deep breath and asked her for the quarter. That whole night he tossed and turned, wondering how he was going to provide for his pregnant wife and child over the next four months. The burden rested on him, a twenty-one-year-old still struggling to be a man.

The next morning, he took the quarter to town and bought eight shotgun shells, which he planned to use to kill some rabbits. If he was lucky, he could get as much as fifteen cents for each one. That evening he killed seven rabbits and one quail. He left one rabbit and the quail at the house to eat and sold the rest. He then bought eight more shells for twenty-five cents and shot some more rabbits.

On the way back to the house, he ran into Rev. Lionel Nelson, who had been his school principal. Nelson saw the rabbits and told Fred he needed some for the girls' cooking class at school, and that if he killed forty for him, he would pay a dime each. Realizing he might not always get fifteen cents for each rabbit, Fred took Nelson up on his offer. The reverend suggested Fred get some fellows in the area to help. But Fred reasoned he didn't need any help, and plus, it would cut into his earnings. The skills he'd learned from Papa about rabbit hunting paid off. In two and a half days, he delivered the forty rabbits to Nelson and received four dollars, which was enough to buy food for his family through the winter. Somehow, they were surviving.

Still, the little money they made from picking and hunting wasn't enough to buy clothes. One time, Fred had to swallow his pride and try to borrow fifteen dollars from the boss man to get Ernestine a dress for church and some things for the baby. Borrowing straight cash from Thum was unheard of, since he never gave money. But he was willing to take a chance.

It just so happened that Ennis Reed, another black man who lived on the farm, was also planning to ask Thum for a loan. So the two of them decided they would go together around noon on Saturday. But instead of waiting for Fred as they agreed, Ennis went and saw Thum early that morning. When Fred saw Ennis on his way back after meeting Thum, he asked what had happened. He said old Thum had given him what he wanted. Fred perked up and almost ran the rest of the way into town.

When he saw Thum, he told him why he needed the money, thinking he would sympathize with him because of the baby. He was wrong. Thum said he wouldn't lend him any money, but he would take an order with the usual 25 percent interest. Trying to be humble, Fred told him he preferred the money. But again the old man refused and told him he'd have to do like the other niggers. Thinking Thum had given Ennis cash but was refusing to do the same for him, Fred almost let him know what he could do with his money. But in the end, he just walked away.

He could feel the tears forming in his eyes from anger and the thought of having to tell Ernestine he wouldn't be able to buy her that dress or clothes for the baby. After he'd walked a few feet, he heard Thum call him: "Little Red, come on back here." Fred turned around and began walking back, keeping his head slightly down to hide the tears that had seeped through. Surprisingly, Thum gave him the fifteen dollars. Fred thanked him and left. As he was walking away, he heard Thum mumble, "Niggers always trying to show off." The comment fired him up, but he was just glad to have the money and didn't look back. When he got to the store, he saw Ennis with a long piece of paper and no money. Thum had given him an order.

About a year later, in 1938, Ernestine gave birth to another boy. They named him Marvin, a cute little fellow with a long head, just like Fred. A third son, named Roy, was born not long after. But he lived only a month. It was a blessing in a way, because he was born with a birth defect that caused him to have spasms all the time and to be in constant pain. The doctors couldn't do anything to help him. When Fred and Ernestine got the news, Fred went outside and prayed. "Lord, if it's your will, let this child live," he said. "But if it isn't, please put him out of his misery." Roy died about twenty minutes later.

In addition to the money Fred was getting from his odd jobs, the government had started issuing subsidies to farmers. Fred was now able to put his dream of owning a house into motion. A man named William Taylor owned an old hall, and he told Fred he would take fifty dollars as down payment and another fifty by that fall. They made the deal, and Fred began renovating the hall into a four-room house, with help from a fellow named Bully Green.

Thum got upset when he found out that Fred was in the process of buying a house. He had noticed for the past couple of years that Fred hadn't been coming to him for orders, which meant he was making enough money to take care of all his family's needs. While Fred was picking cotton in the field one day, Thum walked up to him and pointed his finger in his face, so close Fred could smell the molasses he had sopped that morning. "You makin' too much damn money on my land," he said, turning red as a beet.

Fred replied, "This is your land, and more than half of my profit goes to you. All I'm trying to do is produce a good crop. But if I work the mule too hard, you get mad. If I don't work hard enough, you call me lazy. What do you want me to do, Mr. Thum?"

Having nothing to say, Thum stormed off in silence.

Just as dark, ominous clouds are signs of an imminent storm, Fred knew that incident with Thum was an indication of something very bad to come if he didn't hurry up and move. He almost didn't make it—or rather, old man Thum almost didn't make it.

Fred was plowing the land where he had just cut down a bunch of trees. Sometimes the tiller could cut through a stump, but he hit one that was too tough and bent the axle. Thum was out of town at the time, but Fred knew he'd be back sometime that day. So he got on one of the farm's mules and went into town to get the axle fixed.

On his way back, he ran into Thum, who bitterly questioned why he went to town on his mule. Fred told him what had happened, and that he was there to get the axle fixed. As usual when he got mad, Thum mumbled something under his breath and drove off. Although Fred couldn't quite understand what Thum said, he could make out a few cusswords and the derogatory "nigger." Fred was heated. *Here I am trying to help the man and yet I get cussed?*

It was getting dark, so he decided to wait till the next day to put on the new axle. He had also decided he wasn't going to put up with the old man's insults anymore. *It was time somebody stood up to him.* Fred planned to take a shotgun with him to the field when he went to fix the axle, and if Thum cussed him, he was going to end him.

The next morning, Fred got up earlier than usual so Ernestine wouldn't see him get his gun. She knew he was angry, because he had told her what had happened before they went to bed. She also knew he wasn't going hunting the next morning. If she saw him with the gun, she would know it wasn't rabbits he would be hunting but Thum-hide.

As Fred was walking out the door, he spotted a cat chasing one of the chickens. Without thinking, he raised his gun and flipped that cat like a pancake. Ernestine heard the shot and woke up. But by the time she got to the door, he was already in the field, heading to the tiller. Then she saw Thum's truck pass by the house going in the same direction. Thum had apparently been watching him. Immediately, Ernestine fell on her knees and began to pray.

When Thum showed up, Fred was just about to replace the axle. He had hidden the gun in some loose dirt by the tiller. But to his surprise, Thum didn't utter one cussword. As a matter of fact, he bent down and helped him. "Here, Little Red, let me give you a hand," he said kindly, almost as if he knew his life depended on his tongue. After they fixed the tiller, not saying anything to each other the entire time, he got back in his truck. Before driving off, he leaned out the window and said, "Well, Little Red, I guess you're good to go."

As Fred watched him leave, he was ashamed. Here he had been contemplating killing Thum, but Thum had gotten dirtier than he had fixing the axle. Fred knew he had to leave, soon, before he did anything he would regret.

It was no secret that Fred was hotheaded when it came

to whites and their treatment of blacks. Although he tried to control it, his family—Ernestine in particular—was most familiar with his attitude. Because he and those close to him had been treated inhumanely for so many years, his antipathy toward whites had reached a boiling point. It had turned into sheer hatred.

To help out financially, Ernestine sold candy. Although Fred didn't really want her to, he let her because they could definitely use the money. Once a person reached a certain quota, that individual was entitled to a prize, and Ernestine was due one. But when the man for whom she was selling the candy came by to collect his share of the money, he refused to give her anything, saying she hadn't sold all her candy, which was her quota. Ernestine knew he was just trying to shortchange her. Obviously upset, Ernestine ran to Fred when she saw him coming up the old dirt road leading to their house.

"That old man don't want to give me my prize," she said sobbing. "He said I didn't sell everything."

Fred couldn't stand to see Ernestine cry. More than that, he hated to see her taken advantage of by some old white man. He knew the truth. He had helped her sell the candy—all of it. He ran inside the house, jumped over the bed, and grabbed his shotgun. By the time he came out, the man was getting in his car to leave.

Fred rushed over to the car, shotgun at his side, and yelled, "What the hell is the matter with you? Why don't you give my wife what she earned?"

"I haven't said I wouldn't give it to her," the man replied, now turning pale.

"She said different," Fred replied. By this time he had the barrel of the shotgun inside the window and was nudging the man with it. "Get out and get it. Now!" Fred ordered.

The man nervously hopped out of the car and went to his trunk. He pulled out the prize—a package of kitchen utensils—and handed it over.

"Now you get out of here," Fred said.

In his panicky state, the man tapped his gas pedal several times before trying to start the car, flooding it. But Fred was unaware of what had happened. When he saw that he wasn't leaving, he stuck the shotgun back in the window and demanded, "You can go, can't you?"

Finally the car started, and down the road it flew, shooting out smoke and kicking up dust. Once again, Fred had let his hatred get the best of him. He didn't realize just how deep it ran in his bloodline until a new minister at his church told him a little of his family history.

One day, after service at New Hope C.M.E., Rev. H. C. Walker told Fred he had something he wanted to share with him and asked if he would come by his house. After they had dinner, Walker told Fred that he had been raised by the Montgomerys in Sardis, Mississippi, in the early 1900s, and that he knew Fred's father's father, Ed Montgomery.

Walker said Ed was tall and muscular, even in his old age, and he was known in the area for his fistfights. At a certain time of the year Ed would get drunk and walk to the main road, then flag down vehicles with two or three white men in them and pick a fight. Many times he would get beat up and have to be carried into the house bloodied. But, as if possessed, he kept going back to the road. Walker explained why.

When Ed and his younger brothers, Frank and Richard, were in their early to late twenties, their younger sister was kidnapped by three white men and raped by one of them. She managed to escape and run back home half naked and bleeding. The brothers then went into town, and when they found the man who had raped their sister, they killed him. A riot followed, and the three brothers were forced to hide in an old, run-down house in a wooded area several miles outside of town. They were found after about a month, and when they tried to run, Frank was shot in the back and killed. Ed and Richard managed to escape, but they vowed never to see each other again for fear they might also be killed. They never reunited. Ed took his bitterness and anger to his grave.

Fred thought long and hard about what he'd been told. He was certain he didn't want to die with anger in his heart like his grandfather. That night, before going to bed, he prayed, asking God to help him be forgiving. He remembered his maternal grandmother, Callie, telling him that God "wants us to pray for even our enemies, and forgive them."

Fred knew it wouldn't be easy. But he trusted God would help him.

• • •

When I saw *Roots* for the second time, I was old enough to fully understand what I was seeing. It stirred up feelings of anger within me.

By this time in my life, I had experienced racism, such as the incident in the twenty-four-hour restaurant. I had read about slavery in high school and college history books. And I have seen numerous pictures that disturbed me. Probably the most memorable was the one of a burned body hanging from a tree. I found myself getting angry with the white teachers and their efforts to dissect the time period, often showing little sensitivity to the horrific conditions of African Americans. No matter how much I tried, I couldn't move past this anger.

It was Fred, several years later, who helped me change my perspective and move on. Instead of stewing over what had happened to my ancestors, he suggested I look at the strength and determination they possessed to endure their situation. When I thought about their perseverance, I remembered the words of a spiritual I once heard:

> I don't feel no ways tired
> I come too far from where I started from
> Nobody told me that the road would be easy
> I don't believe He brought me this far to leave me.

Tirelessness. Relentlessness. Alex Haley's *Roots* probably best depicted the unquenchable spirit of blacks in the character of Kunta Kinte, who, despite having half his foot chopped off, continued to run. He wasn't going to let anything stop him from getting his freedom. And there was the unmitigated courage of the African woman depicted in the character known as Kizzy. After being torn from her parents and worked like an animal, she was raped and forced to breed so more of her children would have to come into the world and drink from the bitter cup of slavery. I developed a new respect for black women after seeing her courage. Despite the terrible circumstances that shadowed them daily, some chose to marry and willingly procreated. Still, there were others who spit in the face of procreation. Fred shared such a story with me.

He was giving a tour one day and had reached the part where one of Alex Haley's ancestors, a blacksmith named Tom, was tied to a tree and whipped. A picture of his back showed how the whip had cut into his flesh like butter. As the museum crowd moved on, Fred noticed a young woman crying. It didn't seem unusual at first, because many people became emotional during the tour. But this woman began to sob uncontrollably to the point that Fred asked what was troubling her. After calming down and taking a few deep breaths, the woman said she had learned a few months earlier that her great-great-great-grandmother had killed seven of her children. She was about to kill another when some of her relatives found out and stopped her. Asked why she would do such a thing, the woman ripped open her blouse and showed them the scars on her back. She had been beaten and raped. The woman said she'd rather see her children dead than see them endure the same. "I don't want any of my children to die at the hands of the white man's whip," she said.

Today, slavery has a legacy: racism. Because I detest its origins, it would seem fitting for me to hate its perpetrators. But Fred taught me that hatred is unhealthy. "You have to try to forgive and rise above the hatred," he said. "If not, hate will kill you."

According to Fred, those who harbor hatred and anger should harness those feelings and turn them into a source of motivation to combat racism. He said the torch had been passed from my ancestors to my generation to keep lighting the way along a path that was forbidden to them. The path that leads blacks to institutions of higher learning to attain the knowledge necessary to become teachers, judges, and politicians who can make changes that will promote equality.

We should all empower our younger brothers and sisters to become leaders by taking them back from the streets and directing them toward this path. We need to let them know that before their ancestors were slaves, they were kings and queens in Africa. And that they, too, are royalty. Fred said this is what the Kunta Kintes, the Harriet Tubmans, and the Marcus Garveys would have wanted, and they would be proud of how far we have come. Yet, they would also see room for improvement.

Granted, there's still a lot of work to be done in our fight against racism, still a long and rugged road to travel. But I'm up for the challenge. Because, as I move ever forward, my soul is emblazoned with the fervor of those who went before me.

And I don't feel no ways tired.

CHAPTER 7

THIS LAND, GOD'S LAND, MY LAND

You can't separate peace from freedom because no
one can be at peace unless he has his freedom.
—MALCOLM X

Anytime one man considers killing another man, it's time for
one of them to move. Fred had talked about it, and now he
was really going to do it. Besides, he and Ernestine needed a
bigger place. About a year after Roy's death, they had another
boy, Fred III.

For a long time, Fred did housework on the side for an
elderly black woman named Ms. Dora Diggs. She was a kind,
gentle woman, and they became close friends. She was in her

eighties and a massive stroke had crippled her. She was finding it more and more difficult to do things around the house, as well as certain personal things for herself. So one day she asked Fred if he and Ernestine would consider living with her, and help her pay the back taxes on the house, which her illness had caused her to get behind on. They agreed.

By this time, Bully Green had finished renovating the hall, and it was now a four-room house. When Ernestine and Fred moved in with Ms. Diggs, they decided to give the house to Ernestine's parents. They would never have to worry about anybody putting them out again. Best of all, they were finally off Thum's farm. Even though Fred was now farming for another man, Mr. Willie Lipscomb, he didn't mind, at least not too much anyway. Mr. Lipscomb wasn't at all like Thum. He was fair, and he never cursed. But still, in Fred's eyes, he was a white man.

Ms. Diggs soon died from a second stroke. However, right before her death, she deeded the house to Fred and Ernestine. It was 1940, and they finally had their own home. They stayed there for several years, and during that time had six more children, all about a year apart. Jerdine was the first of that group; they finally had a girl, and she was feisty like her mama and just as lovely. Then came Henry, Ella, Larry, Derik, and Sheila. Two others were stillborn, unlike Roy, who had been a month old. They now had nine children—including Charles, Marvin, and Fred III—and had buried three.

Fred thanked God for giving him his own home. But just as he'd always tried to be somebody and better his life, he also wanted more for his family. He felt that God, too, wanted him to have the best. That meant he had to be totally free, living on his own land. As kind as Mr. Lipscomb was, he was still the boss man, and Fred was still working for him. There was also the fear that something could happen to Mr. Lipscomb and his replacement might be someone like Thum, or Mr. Lewis who made Fred miss school to work in the fields. His boys were now old enough to go to school, and he didn't want anything to get in the way of their education.

At the age of twenty-five, Fred got a job working on the Illinois Central Railroad, making $2.22 an hour. He was overlooked at first because of his small stature. Although he was stocky, he was only about five feet five. Most of the other guys were taller and more robust. But Fred convinced the railroad managers he was a hard worker and could do just about anything other men could do. He evidently proved himself because he got the job. He worked diligently at the railroad until he got the call from Uncle Sam.

World War II had started, and young men were being called to serve. Many whites didn't think blacks were smart enough, alert enough, or brave enough to fight in the war. They apparently had forgotten that blacks had fought courageously and with distinction in the Revolutionary War, World War I, and just about every other war and conflict ever waged by the United States. The black press, the National Association for the Advancement of Colored People (NAACP), and the Congress of Racial Equality made sure the strength and success of blacks were not overlooked. Their constant pressure on the War Department and President Franklin D. Roosevelt's administration to have black soldiers serve equally with white soldiers helped pass the Selective Training and Service Act, which said: "In the selection and training of men under this act, there shall be no discrimination against any person on account of race and color."

Fred was ordered to report to the courthouse in Ripley, and from there he was to leave for basic training. On the day of his departure, he hugged and kissed Ernestine and the children, not knowing whether he would see them again. As he walked toward the door, Ernestine came up behind him and embraced him tightly. When he turned around and saw the tears in her eyes, it was hard for him to let her go. But he pushed her away gently and told her he would be fine, and that he'd be back. He gave her one last embrace, then turned and walked out the door. Ernestine held on to his fingers until the very last moment. She and the children watched as he got in his ride to catch the local train to Ripley. They were now left with only his promise to return. He had never broken a promise to them before, and they hoped this wouldn't be the first.

When Fred got to the courthouse, he waited with about fifty other men for his name to be called. Then he reported to the front desk, where he was given his exact orders. He was listed in what was called Class I, which was to be the first group to leave. However, when his name was called and he approached the man at the desk, he found out that he had been deferred indefinitely. He was surprised by the news. And Ernestine didn't know what to think when she answered the door and there stood her husband just a few hours after he had left. She and the children joyously hugged him.

Fred never got a letter reversing the deferment. He really did want to fight and show those whites what he could do. But he liked being back with his family. And, evidently, God had other plans for him. He returned to the cotton fields and the railroad. At the railroad he was at an advantage: he could read. If there was an order and the supervisor was not around, he would explain it to the other men. The same applied when an equipment broke down and they had to read the instructions to repair it. Fred would read them and show the men how to fix it. The bosses liked that.

One day Fred noticed two narrow strips of land along the railroad that nobody seemed to be using. He mentioned the land he saw to one of his bosses and asked if he could buy it. His boss said he would check with the headquarters in Chicago and let him know. He gave Fred the okay, but informed him that there was a man letting his cows graze on the land, so he would have to tell the man to move them to another area. That man, of all people, turned out to be Sam Thum. The two met once again, and when they did, Thum, as expected, wasn't too nice.

"Don't you come here tellin' me what I need to do," Thum grumbled, his voice cracking from old age and a bitter heart. "If you touch that land, you gonna get a buzzard picking on you."

In a calm voice, Fred replied, "I've got to die sometime." He then turned and walked away.

The following week, Fred learned that Thum had gotten

together with some other businessmen in town and threatened to sue the railroad if they let Fred buy the land. The railroad later sent Fred a letter saying they couldn't sell it to him, but they would rent it to him if he wanted. The letter also said he would be given the first right to purchase if they ever decided to sell. Fred accepted.

About a month later, Fred took some money from his savings and bought a mule to plow the land, so he could plant cotton. He made a good profit that year, which he used to rent more land and buy three more mules. His sons were now big enough to help him, so his workload became a little lighter. Pretty soon he was averaging nearly twenty bales of cotton a year at about $120 each. That number then became thirty, allowing him to save quite a bit.

Then Fred found out that a man by the name of Ed Vaughn had a thirty-seven-and-a-half-acre farm he wanted to sell for $5,000 and was looking for only $1,000 down. Fred went to meet him, and Mr. Vaughn told him he could pay the rest over ten years. Fred and Ernestine took all the money they made from that year's crop plus some of their savings and made the down payment. Their task now was to pay it off, which Fred was determined to do in two years.

As he had always done, Fred killed rabbits and did other odd jobs in the wintertime. But this time around he had more vigor. It was almost as if he could sense the feelings of his ancestors, who toiled on the plantations and worked even harder when they knew their chance at freedom was coming. When they wouldn't have to answer to anybody but themselves. When death would no longer be their only means of freedom.

Fred plowed from sunrise until around four in the afternoon, when the boys would get home from school and relieve him. Watching his family work, he realized just how much they all shared his dream, especially Ernestine. One day the two of them decided to take a break and have dinner under a tree. When he got up to get back to work, he looked over and saw that Ernestine had fallen asleep. She looked so peaceful, and at the same time so beautiful, that he didn't have the heart to wake her. So he went back to the field by himself. As he started plowing, he saw Ernestine heading toward him. Staggering slightly, she picked up the hoe and started to work alongside him. He told her she could stop if she wanted to, but she insisted on staying. Together they worked under the heat, which had to be at least ninety-five degrees.

They made one $2,000 payment by the end of the first year, and by the end of the second year, they had enough to make the final $2,000. When Fred took the money to Mr. Vaughn, he told him he didn't have to give him all of it now but could take longer if he wished. Fred kindly refused the offer and gave him the final payment. He got back to the field where Ernestine was working and showed her the receipt that said PAID. He told her, "Our boys will now be able to go to school when they want to and get a good education. They won't have to answer to anybody but me and you." They knelt down on their farm, on their land, and said a prayer of thanks.

In 1949, Fred decided to quit his job at the railroad and

spend all his time working on the farm, which had become prosperous. Two years after paying it off, he bought two tractors and a Chevy pickup; owned one hundred acres, renting out half of it; and hired some sharecroppers, whom he treated like family. When he had the time, he even did plumbing work, something he'd learned in his teen years working at the local ice plant, for some of the local folks.

Everything was going well, and Fred was proud of all his success. But mainly that he finally had his own plot of land. For that, he was immensely grateful.

• • •

Before he died, my grandfather Daddy Roy stressed the importance of owning property. It was a great joy for him to be able to leave land to his children—land they could pass on from generation to generation. Like him, I remember Fred describing his elation after purchasing his own land. "All the sweat and tears had paid off," he said. "In so many ways, we were free."

As a teenager I remember dreaming of one day owning some property. My mother's voice often made me wish I could expedite that dream. "As long as you're in this house, you'll do as I say," she'd yell whenever I failed to do something she wanted.

At the time, like many youths, I thought my mother was nagging me. But now that I'm older, I realize she just wanted me to be disciplined, to be assertive, and to do well in school.

"If you learn it, they can't take it away from you," she often told me. She wanted me to go further than she and my father had. My sisters, Cathy and Stephanie, graduated at the top of their high school classes, went on to get their master's degrees, and eventually purchased their own homes. Their success and independence are sources of inspiration for me even today.

Toward the end of high school, I made my parents extra proud by graduating with honors. I had always been fascinated with flying and the military, so I endeavored to make the US Air Force Academy my place of higher learning. I received a congressional nomination, but my less-than-perfect eyesight precluded me from becoming a pilot. Not giving up, I decided to major in aerospace at Middle Tennessee State University. I did well my first semester, but I didn't have the money for private pilot lessons. That's when I realized God had something else in store for me.

I decided to pursue my second love, which was writing. I talked to an adviser in the journalism department who directed me to numerous private scholarships available in the field. By the end of my junior year, I had earned enough scholarships to get my own apartment off campus. That summer I got an internship with the *Tennessean*, and the following summer I was able to get one with the *St. Petersburg Times* in Florida. By the time I graduated in 1991, I had enough experience to land an internship with the Associated Press, which turned into a permanent position. I had found my career.

Now that I had a stable income, my sister Cathy suggested I stop paying rent and invest in a house. I agreed. It was time for me to become a homeowner. After selecting a house from a brochure of homes, I discovered that the builder was right around the corner from where I lived. Once they ran a credit check and received the down payment, the construction began. In a little over six months, I moved in.

I was so excited to have my own place that I kept one of the bricks and shingles left over from the construction as if I were collecting souvenirs from some faraway ancient ruins. My greatest joy came when I invited my parents over for the first time. I could tell they were proud of their twenty-three-year-old son, especially my mother. She couldn't stop smiling when she walked inside and saw how neatly I had decorated it. She had a hard time believing that the house belonged to the same child she had to threaten to wash the dishes and take out the trash. Her only complaint was that I had a picture of black writers from the Harlem Renaissance hanging above my dining room table. Granted, it could have been somewhere else. But I liked it where it was.

"That picture just doesn't look right there," she said. "If you're going to hang something near that table, it should have flowers in it, or fruit."

Smiling slightly, I told her, "Mom, I love you and respect you. But I'm not in your house anymore. I pay the mortgage here."

She shook her head. Then, with a smile she herself couldn't hide, replied, "You're right, son. You do."

That evening my parents and I sat around the dining room table and laughed and talked in the company of Langston Hughes, W. E. B. DuBois, and a bunch of other prominent black folks—in my house.

Thanks to the perseverance and diligence of men like Fred, it has become easier for men like me to achieve the dream of owning a home.

CHAPTER 8

WHY, LORD?

Although the world is full of suffering,
it is also full of the overcoming of it.
—**HELEN KELLER**

S unday evenings in the early summer were Fred's favorite time to relax. Sometimes after church he'd come home and sit in the living room with the windows open, or on the porch listening to the radio, and enjoy an occasional cool breeze as the sun set. This quiet time allowed him to reflect on his life, his family, and everything he had gained in his nearly fifty years of living.

On this particular evening in 1963, one of his favorite songs, "Jesus, Keep Me Near the Cross," was playing on the Christian station. He listened intently with his eyes closed, meditating on the words. It almost felt as if God were preparing him for something. Then, suddenly the phone rang, and he got the news.

"Henry has drowned!" yelled a sobbing voice on the other end.

Henry, his sixth child, was a smart, energetic young man whom Fred had planned to send to trade school to become a master plumber. How was Fred to know that his plan for his nearly eighteen-year-old son would be cut short? He stood there, holding the phone in disbelief. Then the caller, Geraldine Harding, a family friend, told him where it had happened and that he needed to get there right away.

It was Keller Lake, about a mile outside of town. On his way there, Fred decided to go and get Ernestine, who was at a missionary meeting at church. He kept thinking to himself, *How am I going to tell her? God, please help me.* When he arrived, she was coming out of the church. She was smiling and talking with the other members as if she didn't have a care in the world. She could read Fred like a book, however, and the look on his face showed what his heart felt. Taking a deep breath, he told her what had happened, and she started screaming and running. He chased her down and pulled her back to the car, where she passed out. He took her home, and a few of the church members came along to help watch her.

When Fred drove up to the lake, there were a lot of people standing around. The police told him they still hadn't found Henry's body and that they were about to drag the lake again. He heard the words, but everything lost their meaning. He just stood there in that one spot, staring at the watery grave of his son. The rescue workers were using giant hooks to drag the lake. Then one of them indicated that the hooks had grabbed on to something. Within a matter of minutes, a limp body was brought up to the top of the water. It was Henry. Even as Fred watched them carry his body to the ambulance, he couldn't believe his son was dead. His son looked as if he were only sleeping, as though he'd respond if Fred just called his name as he had done so many times before in the mornings, in the evenings, and at night. No voice would be heard in response this time. Even worse, Fred wouldn't be able to tell him what he always felt but was never able to say: that he loved him.

The ambulance pulled away with Henry's body and people began to leave. But Fred just stood there in a daze. After a while, a close friend, Neely Johnson, put her arm around him and guided him back to his car. When he got home, the doctor had just given Ernestine a shot to relax her nerves.

About three days later, Fred managed to get Ernestine up for Henry's funeral, and some of her friends came by to help her get ready. She was still in a complete stupor. On the way, she would say every so often, "Henry is gone. My Henry is gone," then weep. Every tear cut into Fred's heart. But he knew he had to be strong for her and refused to let her see him cry. As they walked into the packed church, Ernestine turned to the people sitting at the ends of the pews, and as she passed them, she somberly expressed her pain: "You just don't know. You just don't know."

Nobody could really know the pain Fred's family felt. Ernestine stayed in bed for almost a month following the burial. And it was a while before the rest of the kids were back to normal. Fred had to be strong for everybody. To try to ease his mind, he threw himself into his work. When that wasn't enough, he got involved in local politics. He ran for—and won—a seat as an alderman. It felt good to talk for his neighbors and get things done for his community. Yes, things were getting a little better. But he couldn't help but think, *If something like this happens to one of mine again, I don't know what I'll do.*

Sometimes life can be cruel. Sometimes it seems as if God isn't there. But God is, and he never gives anyone more than they can bear without also providing the strength to make it through. It took another loss for Fred to see that God is never far away.

It was a bitterly cold day in January 1978. But weather didn't really matter much when it came to hunting, which was something Fred did all the time. He would do it in almost any kind of weather. So that day, Fred, Fred III, son-in-law Robert Lee Mosby, and their friends Charles and Larry Halliburton decided to go rabbit hunting on Shoaf Island, about twenty miles west of Henning near the Mississippi River. When they were in their boat heading back to camp down the river, the water was rough, and it was so cold that splashes froze instantly and fell like rock fragments. Big chunks of ice the size of couches floated around the five of them and their five hunting dogs.

The water seemed to get rougher as they floated on down. Then, suddenly, a strong current caused the boat to shift, throwing the men to one side. It capsized, forcing all of them into the water. One of the dogs immediately jumped on Fred's back and pulled off his life preserver. His son pushed an empty gas barrel that had fallen from the boat toward him to hold on to. In a matter of minutes, Fred felt the frigidness of the water, which was in the teens. His bottom half was starting to go numb. By then the dogs were turned on their backs and going under.

His son and Robert Lee said they were going to swim to the bank and get help. They didn't have but a few feet to go. However, within minutes, Fred heard his son calling for help. Then a deathly silence. He looked around and saw that Robert Lee had managed to grab on to the side of the boat that had resurfaced bottom-side up, but he couldn't see his son.

Having lost sight of Fred III and their friends, they were now alone. In the cold and darkness, Fred held on to the barrel and Robert Lee to the boat as chunks of ice bounced off their bodies. They began to drift in and out of consciousness. Fred's confidence was failing him, and he knew death was now a strong possibility. But he wasn't afraid. As always, his concern was for Ernestine. He just prayed God would strengthen her, so that she would be able to handle the loss. His thoughts were suddenly interrupted by scratching, then a gurgling sound. Then, again, there was silence. With as much breath as he could muster, Fred called out, "Robert Lee! Robert Lee!" When he got no answer, he knew his son-in-law was dead. Pretty soon, Fred started to lose consciousness. But before he did, he saw a boat approaching with what looked like two men wearing black hoods. That's the last thing he remembered seeing before blacking out completely.

Fred woke up in the hospital. A white doctor standing over him was apologizing because he had to slap Fred a few times to help him regain consciousness. He told him he was lucky to be alive. He had been in the water almost an hour and was comatose for nearly three hours. The nurse gave him some medicine, and Fred went back to sleep. He awoke a second time to find another white man standing over him. He was a somewhat tall fellow, with an eerily calm look on his face. Fred was a little startled at first, but then the man told him who he was and what he had done. A chill went down Fred's spine as he listened.

The man said he was one of the two men Fred saw approaching before he blacked out. He and his hunting companion had pulled him out of the river. What stuck with Fred the most was that the man was a preacher. *God's best man saved my life*, Fred thought.

The preacher said he hadn't planned to go in Fred's direction, but something compelled him to change his course. When he found Fred, he was as stiff as a board. Fred's glasses were frozen to his ears, but he was afraid to remove them in case he pulled Fred's ears off. He then ran to some of the houses along the river to get help, collecting blankets, sheets, and anything else people could give to put around Fred and Charles Halliburton, the other man they were able to rescue. With the residents' help, they managed to take the two men back to their trucks and turn on the heat until the paramedics arrived.

Just when Fred was about to ask him if he knew anything about the other three, one of Fred's daughters, Sheila, walked in. He asked her about his son. She first said he was okay, but then broke down in tears. Fred knew he didn't make it. He later found out that Charles's brother, Larry, also perished.

When Fred got home from the hospital, Sheila had made up a bed downstairs for him to sleep. But instead he went into one of the rooms upstairs and fell on his knees. With both hands in the air and tears running down his face, he wanted to ask, *Why, Lord? Where do I go from here?* But he was too choked up to make a sound. He just knelt there, humming the song "Precious Lord, Take My Hand." He tried to release the pain through the streams of tears that didn't seem to end. The tears he never allowed himself to shed for Henry fifteen years earlier were now joined with those for Fred III.

Following the funerals, life was painful. Fred III and Robert Lee were the backbone of the family plumbing business. They drove two of the three trucks Fred operated. He felt as though both his arms had been cut off. Some days he didn't feel like doing anything. And when he did go back to work, he struggled. Gloom seemed to be all around him, literally. At times he'd look up and a mist would be following him wherever he went. One day, he decided he just couldn't take it anymore.

He got in his pickup truck and headed for the bridge leading out of town. Once on the bridge, he pushed the accelerator to the floor and tried to drive over the side. But the steering wheel wouldn't turn. After he had crossed the bridge, though, the wheel miraculously unlocked. He thought it was just a fluke and that it wouldn't happen again. He decided he would make sure of it that night.

After tucking a copy of his will under his pillow, Fred slipped outside quietly so Ernestine wouldn't hear him. He got behind the wheel of his car and again headed for the outskirts of town. When he got to the railroad tracks, he glanced at his watch. It was around eight thirty, and the train was scheduled to pull through at nine o'clock. He drove his car right up onto the rails, put it in park, and turned off the engine. Now all he had to do was wait for the whistle in the distance. He would then see the locomotive bearing down on him, and it would be over.

He sat in the driver's seat staring down the tracks, listening for the nine o'clock whistle. Nine o'clock came and went. Then nine fifteen. He'd never known the trains to be late; you could practically set your watch by them. Yet it had not come through. By nine thirty he began to worry that someone might see his car on the tracks and get suspicious. So he decided to move it, then go back and sit on the tracks. While he was parking the car behind some bushes, there was a loud whistle and the train zoomed by.

There's another one due at ten, he thought. *I'll just catch that one. It won't be late again.*

At nine forty-five, he walked to the railroad track and sat down on a tie. Ten o'clock came and went, but the train did not. Around ten forty-five, he finally gave up and headed back to his car. Just then, he heard a whistle as the train whizzed by. He couldn't believe it.

He went back home, and there he again fell on his knees and cried out, "Why, Lord? As old as I am, you let me live but didn't spare those young men. I don't understand. Why?" He prayed long and hard, but he could not come up with a reason. He cried himself to sleep, with his will still under his pillow.

The next morning, he awoke to see the sun he hadn't expected to see the day before. Still somewhat dazed and heavy-laden from crying nearly all night, he slowly dressed to go into town. Once there, the strangest thing happened. Nearly every person he encountered had something nice to say about his son or some other words of comfort. Everyone. Even the grown white men he'd always thought hated him because he was black. He realized all those white people didn't hate him. That they, too, had experienced a painful loss at one time or another and were able to cry for him and with him. As they did, their tears seemed to flood Fred's heart and soul, cleansing him of his grief as well as of the animosity he'd felt toward them for so many years. He had lost several loved ones, but now he had an extended family of brothers and sisters, both black and white.

God made us all, and we're all his children, he realized. Fred also believed that one day he'd find out why God had kept him alive. Like the faith he saw his mother have when he was a child, he just had to "be still, and know" (Ps. 46:10) that God would give him an answer.

"God does things for a reason. One that we will understand by and by. Until then, we must continue to put our trust in him, because he will sustain us," Fred explained.

• • •

During one of my visits to Henning, I stood on the railroad tracks where Fred had attempted to take his life. I faced the direction the train was supposed to have come from that night and tried to imagine it coming at me with its whistle blaring and tons of steel crashing into my body. It was unfathomable. I couldn't imagine committing suicide.

My mother and grandmother always said, "God will never put more on you than you can bear." However, the battle between good and evil has been waged since the beginning of time. And the latter wants you to believe that life's blows are too much to bear and that the only means of escape is drugs, alcohol, or the ultimate false sense of freedom—suicide.

Fred saw suicide as a way of escape. "At the time, I couldn't see the pain ending. It didn't seem like it was ever going to ease off," said Fred. "I couldn't sleep. It was like a recurring nightmare, and I just didn't want to endure it any longer." But after God snatched him from death and gave him a new lease on life, he realized God had always looked after him. "God was there all the time. I should have kept trusting in him to take away the pain, because he would have eventually."

I also know the feeling of waiting for the pain to go away all too well, especially in the case of a loved one who's suffering.

My grandfather Daddy Roy had always been leery of doctors. He would say, "They're like mechanics. You take your car to them for one thing, and they find something else wrong."

But he had to go see a few of them after having problems with his vision. He was told he had cataracts in both eyes and needed surgery. But before operating, they took some tests and found blood in his urine. After running further tests, he was diagnosed with prostate cancer. It was the last thing any of us expected.

At first, like many cancer patients, everything was fine. He continued to get up before dawn to farm—feeding his cows, horses, and pigs and tilling the land on his tractor until sunset. Gradually, though, things began to change. His back started to ache, and each day the pain seemed to get worse. Then he lost his appetite. He began to lose weight and was frequently nauseated. He'd always loved my grandmother's homemade biscuits, which she made for breakfast, lunch, and dinner. But Daddy Roy got to the point where he could barely touch them.

We didn't want to face it, but the cancer was spreading, rapidly zapping his livelihood and energy before our very eyes. It all seemed so unfair. This was a man who had always tried to do good. He loved his family and cared for others. In their younger days, he and my grandmother owned a small store, and when times were tough, they would let some customers, including a few whites, have items on credit.

Daddy Roy enjoyed it when everyone would get together and sit around the table at his house, eating and laughing. Visitors were always welcome to join the family for meals. We tried to continue the tradition during his illness, but it just wasn't the same without him. It was tough looking at his empty chair, knowing he was in the back room fighting for his life.

I saw him a few weeks before his death. My mother called and told me I needed to come see him because he probably didn't have much time. When I got there, my aunts and cousins greeted me with hugs and smiles, but their expressions soon faded to worry. It was tough on all of us because my grandfather was such a hard worker, a fighter. I remember stories about how, at age twelve, he drove a log wagon of eight mules and horses to help his mother take care of his three siblings. He maintained that same work ethic his entire life—until cancer forced him down.

As I walked down the hallway leading to his bedroom, it seemed longer than usual, as if I were moving in slow motion. But no matter how much time I took, I don't think anything could have prepared me for what I saw. This wasn't the same man I'd seen about six months earlier. The man before me was much darker, and his skin was wrinkly and loose, as if it had been draped over a skeleton. The cancer had spread to his chest area, filling his lungs with fluid, which hampered his breathing. Some of my relatives took turns helping him cough up phlegm to ease the congestion. I wanted to cry. Dazed, he looked at me, but I don't think he recognized me. I stepped closer, leaned over, and kissed him on the forehead. That was the last time I saw him. He died about two weeks later.

As a result of his losses, Fred said he had a stronger relationship with God, whom he depended on to do everything. As I listened to him talk about his best Friend with joy and sincerity, I was reminded once again of my grandmother, whose belief in God was so strong that she would ask him what clothes to wear before she left the house. I used to laugh at that. But I don't anymore.

"I can do all things through Christ who strengthens me," she often said, quoting Philippians 4:13 (NKJV), one of her favorite scriptures.

Undoubtedly, her faith and love played a big role in the salvation of my grandfather.

CHAPTER 9

NEW LEASE ON LIFE

Courage and perseverance have a magical
talisman, before which difficulties disappear
and obstacles vanish into air.
—JOHN QUINCY ADAMS

About a decade had passed since Fred's brush with death. His own close call as well as the kindness shown by so many whites gave him a new outlook on life. He also made a lot of lifelong friendships through his plumbing business. Many people remembered the care he showed as he did his work. All those years of hard work and compassion helped him win the seat of alderman.

As the alderman, Fred spearheaded the effort to get a $240,000 grant to renovate Bates Street—called the Colored Lane—the poor section of Henning where most of the blacks lived. The money was used to put in a sewer line, install a new gas line, and put a fire hydrant in the area. This won him favor with the people and set him up for his next big political move.

After writing the book *Roots*, Alex Haley became a household name. That gave his hometown of Henning a lot of attention, and his boyhood home was turned into a national museum. Alex and Fred had always been more like brothers than friends, and they remained close even after their boyhood days. So Alex asked Fred to be its curator.

Alex often invited Fred on some of the long trips he took to write. In 1988, he wrote the museum board and asked permission for Fred to sail with him to Japan. At one point during the trip, they struck up a conversation about the upcoming 1988 mayoral election in Henning. There were several prospects, but Alex told Fred he thought Fred should run. Fred replied that he had considered the idea but wasn't sure. For the next ten days, the issue of running weighed heavily on Fred's mind. He prayed about it, then waited for God to give him an answer. He soon got it.

The first thing Fred did when he got back from the trip was meet with some of the blacks who he thought should run. To him, that was the Bates family. He met with three of them—Robert, John L., and Matt—at their house to discuss the need for a black mayor. But they all declined, and instead said, since Fred had been on the board of aldermen the longest, they'd support him. Their slogan was "Together We Stand."

Fred then went around to all the black churches and let them know that he was running. He was surprised to discover how unsupportive some of his own people were. A lot of them were afraid, saying the town wasn't ready for a black mayor. Others simply doubted his ability, saying at age seventy-one he was too old to run. Even though he'd been successful politically as alderman, many thought that with not much education he couldn't succeed as mayor. Then a huge dagger was thrown from the other side. Fred got word from some of the whites that the town didn't need a nigger mayor. But he wasn't about to back down; in fact, the remark just made him even more determined.

Fred went beyond the churches to the gambling dens, and even to Chocolate City, a little juke joint outside of town where blacks went to drink and dance. His supporters held some of their meetings there. The more he went around and talked about the things he would do for the town, the importance of registering black voters, and the timeliness of electing a black mayor, the more it seemed that people were starting to listen and change their minds. They were starting to believe the town could have a black mayor. Many who had sworn they'd never vote began registering.

Fred also made pitches on his plumbing rounds. He was the town's first black master plumber. When he went to the houses of old white widows, Ernestine would go with him because it was still dangerous for a black man to be seen coming out of a white woman's house by himself, no matter how old he was. Some women would call late at night, early in the morning, whenever they had a problem. Ernestine didn't mind accompanying him because she knew it was for his own good. Her job was to talk to the women while Fred worked. One of his favorite clients was Mrs. Agnes Pipkin, a jovial little old white lady who always wore a smile as bright as the sun. She had known Fred most of his life and always trusted him. When he was younger, he was the first black person the Pipkins allowed to work the cash register in their store, Henning Supply, the largest one in town at the time.

One day, as he was leaving her house after doing some plumbing work, Mrs. Pipkin told him, "Fred, I've been knowing you a lifetime, and you just seem to be different. Would you promise me something?"

"Yes, ma'am," Fred said.

"Will you promise me that if I vote for you and get you elected, you won't get uppity and stop coming to see about me like you been?"

"Mrs. Pipkin, I don' think I'll ever forget about you," Fred replied, laughing.

Mrs. Pipkin was one of many whites who promised Fred their vote. Some said they would vote for him but asked that he not tell anybody about it. He promised he wouldn't. Heck, he didn't care if they were two-faced or not, as long as he got their vote. The ballot box didn't discriminate.

Soon it was voting day, and Fred and his campaign rejoiced. Blacks from the Colored Lane flooded the polls. There were people like Jessie Lake, who rolled down in her wheelchair to vote, and Richard Pete, a blind man who had quit voting and swore he'd never vote again. Then there was an eighty-eight-year-old white lady named Mrs. Virginia Tuholski, considered the matriarch of Henning. Her maid helped her to the voting booth, and she told the local newspaper she was voting for Fred

Ernestine in her teens.

Strapping Fred Montgomery
in his early twenties.

Fred and Ernestine many decades later.

Fred (front and center) and other men from New Hope CME Church in 1957.

Fred (far left) singing in New Hope Church men's choir at the opening of the Alex Haley Museum in 1986.

Fred and Alex Haley.

Fred on a freighter
during one of his trips
with Alex Haley.

Fred (left) with Alex
Haley researcher
George Sims (center)
and another friend of
Alex's in Japan.

Fred eating a Japanese meal.

Fred posing with his aldermen shortly after being sworn in as mayor of Henning, Tennessee—the town's first black mayor.

Fred talking with Don Sundquist during his campaign for governor of Tennessee.

A proud Fred holding two of his great-great grandchildren.

The house that Alex Haley bought for Fred and Ernestine.

Fred and Ernestine lead family members in prayer.

The Alex Haley Museum and house in which Alex grew up.

Alex Haley's grandfather,
who built the house that is
now the museum, was one
of the first black businessmen
in West Tennesee.

Alex Haley standing on a
dock in Annapolis, Maryland,
the place he believed his
ancestors arrived from Africa.

The African griot
who holds the
knowledge of
the village in his
head, and the boy
who has to learn
everything the griot
knows.

(Left to Right) Fred's cousin Sis Brooks, Alex's grandma Cynthia, and Alex's aunt Liz, also called Lizzette or Elizabeth. These three women helped nurture Fred and Alex.

Alex Haley's tombstone.

Fred and
Ernestine
in 2003.

Fred talking to author Lucas L. Johnson II in 2003.

Daddy Roy,
Lucas Johnson's
grandfather,
holding Lucas.

because "he's honest." His heart swelled from all the support. Before the voting booths closed, Fred ran into his opponents, two white men. He told them, after much prayer, God had revealed to him that he was going to be the next mayor of Henning. They both laughed. But Fred had the last laugh. The final tally showed he had more votes than both of them put together.

During the time Fred was elected, the mayor of a small town like Henning also had to serve as judge. This was a challenge for Fred. Not so much because of the extra duty but because of problems with his own people as well as whites. Blacks who knew him thought he should let them go with a warning, and some whites simply didn't think an old black man should be telling them what to do. But as he'd always done, Fred met the controversy head-on.

In one case, a teenage boy speeding through Henning at eighty miles per hour was chased by police until he ran off the road and into a cotton field where he got stuck. Police arrested the boy and took him before Judge Fred Montgomery. When some of the townsfolk got word that the boy had been arrested, they were shocked. They knew his father—a mean, burly white man—was a troublemaker, and they felt Fred would be intimidated by him. They thought wrong. When the man came to court with his son, he was huffing and puffing angrily. But Fred told him he should be thankful.

"Wouldn't you rather come down here and pay a fine, than go to a funeral?" he asked.

"Well, I don't really want to do either one of them," the man said.

"Suppose I let him go," Fred continued. "Next time he might get himself killed or kill someone else before he got to where he was going."

The man reluctantly paid the fine.

Fred got all kinds of threats. One person even threatened to burn down his house. But he didn't run and hide. He continued to walk the streets of his town like everybody else. "If they want to burn my house down, let them," he said. "I'll build a new one."

Fred had a reason to be unafraid. He was seventy-one years old, and God had spared his life several times. No man was going to decide when he should leave this earth. Only God would be the judge of that.

• • •

After all Fred had been through, in the end, God showed him that he was in control. Fred simply had to have faith and trust him—just as Fred's mother, Ionie, had done, as did other blacks who called God's name in despair.

Fred didn't run for mayor until he was assured in his heart that God wanted him to do it. Likewise, most of the men in my family saw their mothers, aunts, and grandmothers fall on their knees in prayer when their men needed guidance. The men knew about God, but they didn't have a relationship with him like the women did. That would explain why nine of them—my father and eight others—battled substance abuse. They eventually found peace of mind once they formed that relationship for themselves. They finally understood that they needed to stop looking down on themselves and instead look up to God.

In the case of my father, I must admit, it was weird at first. All of a sudden, around my second year in college, he stopped drinking and started acting like the fathers I'd read about in books or seen some of my friends have. His presence was now constant. When I needed transportation, he helped me get my first car. He seemed like a new man—healthier, livelier. He said he had been sober for a while, but at times I was skeptical. I wanted to accept this new person, but I was afraid I'd be hit with yet another broken promise. I had experienced too many of those as a child to believe it. However, as the years went on, whenever I visited home, I encountered the same sober man each time. *Maybe he changed*, I thought.

We finally talked about it, and he explained what had happened. He said all the times he'd broken his promises to me about drinking and saw the disappointed look on my face, he was heartbroken. He felt trapped. He thought he wouldn't ever be able to stop because he was sick. At one point, he contemplated taking a gun and blowing his brains out. But just as he was about to reach for the gun, he got down on his knees and pleaded with God to remove his taste for alcohol, to "please wipe it from my mouth." By that evening, he had no desire to slip out of the house and go to the liquor store. It was Saturday, then Sunday, no taste. Monday, no taste. Weeks went by, and still he had no urge for even a sip. It's been more than fifteen years, and my father is still sober. His prayer was answered that day.

God also heard the prayers of the other men in my family

who were addicted to everything from heroin to cocaine. They, too, are now sober. The youngest of them, however, is serving the remainder of a fifteen-year prison sentence. He said being incarcerated has disciplined him and helped turn his life around. But when I think about how he ended up where he is, I feel partly responsible.

My cousin Harold was exposed to marijuana as an infant. His father was a supplier of it, and he and Harold's mother were big-time users. When Harold and I were both nine years old, we watched our older cousins get high. They often let Harold take puffs just to see how he would react, but they never let me. They felt Harold was used to it because he had inhaled it since birth. But me—they thought I was smart and that I was going to be somebody, and they didn't want to mess that up. It was as though my and Harold's fates were set in motion by their misconstrued judgments. Even though I was young, I felt guilty for most of my life whenever I thought about how I had just sat there and said nothing. Instead of trying to dissuade Harold of their misconceptions, I watched him through the smoke that was growing between us, dividing us, like an omen of the paths we would later take in life.

As he got older, Harold became more and more locked into the cycle of a drug user. His folks were no help. They both became addicted to crack cocaine, which eventually caused them to break up. His mother skipped town and left Harold with his father. At age sixteen, Harold became a father himself. But because he was in and out of jail, he hardly ever saw his child, named Devin. Harold's father tried to make up for lost time by attempting to raise the little boy and enrolling him in school when he found out Devin wasn't going. However, the addiction got the best of him, and he also ended up in jail. He and Harold served six months together and saw each other often. Can you imagine doing work detail in the cafeteria and watching your father come down the line each day?

Now Devin really had nobody. He was sent back to his mother, who at the time was already taking care of five other children by herself. Meanwhile, Harold was still battling his own demons. He twice tried to overdose on pills but failed. Other family members tried to reach out to him over the years, but he slapped everybody's hands. After burglarizing the homes of two of his aunts, he was involved in a botched drug deal that left him with a charge of second-degree murder. He had now graduated from jail to prison, and it would be his home for a while.

The last time I went to see him, he looked good. He said he'd asked God to forgive him, and that he was continuing to pray and read his Bible. I told him to stay strong. We both pondered why God had spared him from the attempted suicides and other brushes with death. Just as God had a reason for sparing Fred, I believe he also had a purpose for Harold. Perhaps he was to be a testimony, like our cousin Anderson, who let Harold take small puffs years ago.

After not using drugs for some time, Anderson had to appear before one of Memphis's toughest judges for violating his probation, which he received when he was addicted to cocaine. He faced jail time. But after Judge Ann Pugh read an article I'd written in *Essence* magazine about Anderson's recovery and all the positive things he'd been doing, she was moved to tears and dropped the charge against him. (See the complete article in the appendix.)

When Anderson called me at work and told me what had happened, I was in disbelief and jokingly asked him, "You've been smoking again, haven't you?" After getting more details, I realized he wasn't kidding. He said there were others in the courtroom that day crying as well, and that he had an eerie feeling, as if "someone or something unseen was also there."

After the call, the reporter in me had to know more. So I looked up the number for the Shelby County General Sessions Criminal Court to reach Judge Pugh. When I called and told her I had written the *Essence* article, she told me how much it had touched her and why she changed her mind. I asked her if she could send me a letter detailing how she felt that day. She told me her schedule had been "out of control," but that she would send me something. I expected maybe a page, but I got three. Here is part of what she wrote:

> It is really difficult to express what I felt on that last day when Anderson Jackson Jr. appeared before me for final adjudication of his violation of probation charge. Quite honestly, I don't know how to describe my feelings. I know that my reaction was something very out of the ordinary for me. I have been a judge for fifteen years, and during that time I have seen many failures and ruined lives, but I have also seen several successful turnarounds and positive steps. Thus

I cannot really explain why your article about Anderson touched my emotional chords so dramatically. Perhaps it was because I had experienced a long period of time with nothing but bad news, a long dry spell of feeling "What good am I doing here," a long time of no positive reinforcement. But I started reading your article about Anderson silently, at first, and then just started reading it aloud—and over the microphone. Everyone in the courtroom could hear.

The more I read, the more emotional I became—to the point that I could not read at all for the tears that were freely and uncontrollably flowing from my eyes. There was a time of total silence—then I continued reading, my voice quivering. I think the article brought out the hopelessness, the anguish, the total frustration that I feel toward repeat offenders, that family members and friends must feel when their loved ones revert back to the old ways of drugs and crime. And then your article showed that, at least in Anderson's case, there is hope—a bright side. "And every Sunday his mother's face glowed as he walked through the church door" (quoted from your article). I could just see the face of this woman as she saw her son—see the happiness, the hope, the love. And I thought of all the mothers who never experience this—rather they are taken to the morgue to see their son who has been murdered or killed as a result of his lifestyle.

Needless to say, there was a hush over the entire courtroom. I know there were tears in several eyes, including the two court clerks. I told Anderson he should be thankful that he had people who cared enough for him to stick by him, that many of those in the courtroom that day probably did not have anyone who cared what happened to them. I dismissed the violation of probation. And because of just a few such success stories, I shall continue to encourage and *order* probationers to get their high school diplomas, get jobs, go to rehabilitation, go to anger management seminars, or whatever else I feel would help them. It takes a little more time to be concerned, but I do want to be more than just a robot who hands out sentences.[2]

Judge Pugh was right. Anderson has a caring family, a praying family. My father and cousins knew to call on God in their time of need, because they were raised by mothers who called on his name feverishly when they were raising their sons. But our mothers didn't stop there. They prayed even after their sons had left their nests.

Fred's mother and grandmother also never stopped praying.

The last time I saw Anderson, we talked about Harold, and he said something that stuck with me: "We all got him high."

That's true. Little did he and my other cousins know that when they laughed and watched Harold get high years ago, they were sending him on a path to destruction. But we both agreed it wasn't too late to alter the course. Harold is still alive. And one thing is definite: it's better to pull him up as many times as necessary, than to have to lower him once six feet under.

CHAPTER 10

THE GREAT HUSH

The friendship that can cease has never been real.

—SAINT JEROME

Alex Haley would travel to Henning from his home in Knoxville, Tennessee, when he was troubled or just needed to get away. While there, he would visit New Hope Church, a place where he could unload the stress and burdens of the week and allow the minister's sermon to serve as fuel to get through the next five days. Sometimes Fred would sing "Hold to God's Unchanging Hand" for him, which was Alex's favorite song.

One day in spring 1991, Alex was in town to interview his old buddy for a story about his life. He always thought Fred was a fascinating man and the world would be inspired by his trials and triumphs. During the interview, the two got off on the strange subject of burial plots. Alex told Fred that when he passed, he wanted to be buried in the front yard of the Palmer House and asked him if he could get the paperwork started. Fred promised he would. At the time, he didn't see Alex's request as too strange, and he began talking with the state and museum officials to get it done.

The following month, Alex invited Fred and Ernestine to his home in Knoxville, just to get together and talk more about the book. While they were there, Ernestine mentioned that she would like to move. She said she had looked at a few houses and found one in particular that she liked. Then, out of the blue, Alex said he would buy the house for them. They both told him no, that it was out of the question. But they had forgotten about his character. He was a giving man, always looking to do something for others. For instance, when the filming of *Roots* started, Alex approached LeVar Burton, who played Kunta Kinte, and told him it was an extraordinary time in his life and that his mother should be on hand to see it. When Burton told him he couldn't afford to buy the plane ticket for his mother, Alex sent her one.

Alex's generosity toward Fred was even stronger. Since they were boys, he had always seen Fred having to struggle for everything in his life. Now that they were older, and he was able to, Alex wanted to make sure Fred never had to struggle again. That's why Fred shouldn't have been surprised when on Alex's next visit to Henning he brought up the house again. Fred agreed that the house Ernestine liked—an old ten-room, Continental-style home—was beautiful. But, again, he refused when Alex spoke of getting it for them. He had too much pride for that, even if Alex was like a brother to him.

Later, when they stopped by the Alex Haley Museum, Arthilia Sawyer, a worker at the museum and a good friend to them both, overheard their conversation about the house. She pulled Fred to the side once Alex left the room and told him, "He really wants you to have that house, and he's not going to be satisfied until he gets it for you. So please say yes."

Fred thought about it and eventually came up with a compromise. After discussing it with Ernestine, Fred told Alex he would allow him to buy the house for them, but he wanted to assume the payments at some point. Alex agreed. Then he said with a smile, "Well, I'm glad you did come around, because I've already gotten it."

When Fred and Ernestine moved into the house, people came from all over town to see it. Many couldn't understand such love between two people not of the same bloodline. But then, it's possible they didn't know the story Fred once told Alex, which is what fueled Alex's desire to buy the house even more.

When Fred was a teenager, the house was owned by Jack Austin, the town boss and one of the men who had teamed up with Sam Thum to keep Fred from purchasing land from the railroad company. It was also the same house that a young Fred and young Ennis Reed, the one who would later ask Thum for a loan, were passing by when Mrs. Austin yelled out the door and asked them if they wanted to make a dime apiece. They both said yes. When they got up to the front door, she told them to take off their shoes before they came in, then instructed them to move an old antique chest up a spiraling staircase to the second floor of the house. Needless to say, the chest was extremely heavy. But the two boys wanted the money, so they moved the chest as instructed.

It's funny how life brings things back around, then adds a little twist. Not only did Fred go on to become the city's first black mayor, but he ended up living in the house once owned by the town boss. Alex was pleased with what he had done for his buddy. But unfortunately, he wouldn't be around long enough to see him enjoy it.

In February 1992, less than a year after Fred and Ernestine moved into the house, Fred got a phone call informing him that Alex had suffered a massive heart attack and had died. Like when he had gotten the call about the death of his son Henry, he just stood there in shock. It didn't really hit him that Alex was gone until he went to the city hall, where a bunch of reporters and television crews were waiting to talk to him. When the first question about Alex's death was asked, Fred let go and cried uncontrollably. It hit him. His buddy was gone.

There were two memorial services, one in Memphis and one in Henning. Fred hadn't planned to attend the one in Memphis, but Alex's family—his middle brother, George, and others—sent for Fred and Ernestine. At the funeral, there were people from nearly every walk of life—African dignitaries, politicians, and actors. There was a spot in the program where Fred was to speak, but he didn't know what to say. Then George whispered, "Sing, Fred, sing." The only song he could think of was Alex's favorite, "Hold to God's Unchanging

Hand." And he sang it as he never had before. The whole church was moved, to the point many stood up and sang along. When he finished, a white judge, Judge Willard Norvell, ran up to Fred, grabbed him by his arms, and, crying, said he'd never heard anything so moving.

In Henning, after the service at New Hope Church, a flute player from Memphis, who had studied African music, led a procession from the church to the Haley Museum, where Alex had requested to be buried. Fred had left word with some of the church members to start ringing the old town bell when they saw the procession coming, because back when he and Alex were boys, the bell was rung after somebody died.

Max Reynolds, a longtime white resident of Henning, saw the procession as it passed by. He said usually his dogs would bark and whine whenever the bell rang, but this time they didn't make a single sound. Oddly, they stretched their little paws out and put their heads down, almost as if paying respect. He said he couldn't even hear the birds chirping.

He was right. When the bell stopped ringing, there was a great hush, and all that could be heard was the flute player leading the way to the burial site of one of Africa's native sons. One of America's heroes.

• • •

While doing some research to write this book, I came across a photo-essay called *Black Light: The African American Hero*. Created by director Bill Duke, with an introduction by actor

Danny Glover, it highlights a number of individuals who stand out in black history. Among them are Martin Luther King Jr.; Langston Hughes; Malcolm X and his widow, Betty Shabazz; Maya Angelou; and, of course, Alex Haley.

For a long time, such individuals seemed bigger than life, beyond my reach. They were people I saw on television and at the movies or read about in books. But being a journalist provided me with opportunities to contact them and actually speak or meet with them. I had come to realize that they were like everybody else, and some were very personable. I remember talking to Betty Shabazz about her husband before she died and how kind she was during the interview. Then there was the conversation with Danny Glover, who called me back at my home number after I left a message with his publicist. He was so down-to-earth that it was like talking to one of my friends. But it was my correspondence with Maya Angelou that I remember the most.

I had started a magazine during my junior year in college, and I needed a judge for a poetry contest I was sponsoring. I always thought big, so I figured, who was better than Maya Angelou? I got the address of the college where she taught and sent her a letter, not really expecting a response. But within a week, I received a letter. She wrote that she didn't have time to be a judge but wanted to contribute to the prize money and had enclosed a check for $250. She also asked that I keep her informed regarding my life, stating, "I am convinced that you are going to do something marvelous."

Not giving up on finding a judge, and still thinking big,

I sent a letter to Nikki Giovanni. She wrote back saying she could judge the contest. I still have the letters from these two great women I received back in summer 1990. They are not only an inspiration but a lesson that nothing is too big and no one is out of reach.

However, sometimes it may not be necessary to go that far to find great individuals. They may be just a few miles away, around the corner, or right next door. In his introduction to *Black Light: The African American Hero*, Glover describes a hero as a person who transforms the hardship of their experiences into a form of inspiration for others. In short, a hero makes humanly possible what may seem impossible.

One person that comes to mind is my cousin Vernice Armour, a twenty-nine-year-old combat helicopter pilot for the US Marines. She flew numerous missions during Operation Iraqi Freedom in 2003, becoming the first black female fighter pilot for not only the US Marines but the entire US Department of Defense.

Another is Irene Deaner, the grandmother of Devin, my cousin Harold's son. After Harold went to prison and her daughter, an intravenous drug user, died at age twenty-nine, she took on the responsibility of raising Devin and his seven siblings. The children have four different fathers, none of whom provides much help. Irene gets some governmental assistance, but most of the money comes from her personal income, savings, and a few family members.

Then there are the men in my family, and those like them, who have overcome substance abuse. Using is easy. But it takes a real man to stop, fight through the urge, and never look back. Harold's father revived his old upholstery business and has a spot for his son when he gets out of prison. He hopes one day Harold will take over the business. My cousin Anderson, who once pawned his sister's $13,000 car for three rocks of cocaine, has a city job and is saving to buy a house. Another cousin runs his own restaurant. And a cousin who once showed me the holes in his arms from where he shot heroin has a successful career in the military. Then there's my father, Lucas, after whom I'm proud to be named. He's retired from the school system after twenty-eight years of teaching, and he and my mother now live in a house built on land given to him by his father. There are other men in my family who have also found stability. They are all survivors, warriors.

There are other success stories in families all over the world. Alex's book *Roots* tells of the courage and strength of his ancestors despite slavery's horrific grip. Their story inspired millions. There are many others just as encouraging. That's why Alex wanted us to talk to people like Fred Montgomery, storytellers in their own right, who weathered the turbulent times of yesteryear to provide a clearer and better today.

They are the iridescent magic of black light that shines in the dark, illuminating the way. They are our heroes.

CHAPTER 11

LIFE NOW

Every experience God gives us, every person
He puts in our lives, is the perfect preparation
for the future only He can see.

—CORRIE TEN BOOM

A lot has happened since Alex's death. If he were still alive, he would no doubt be moved by the accomplishments of his buddy. In June 2001, at the age of eighty-four, Fred stepped down as mayor after serving twelve years. His accomplishments as mayor are numerous. Most notable was his effort to unite the schools in Henning, which were kept segregated until the early 1970s. He was also instrumental in bringing a new factory to town and building new apartments for low-income and elderly residents.

The same year he stepped down, the town of Henning held a special ceremony honoring Fred Montgomery for his many years of political and community service. A proclamation from the state legislature was read in his honor, and a number of people spoke about the impact he made on their lives. Some of the stories were humorous:

Whenever he could, Fred tried to mentor the young black boys in the community. One of his biggest benefits was giving them part-time jobs in his plumbing business and teaching them a skill. On one occasion, he asked Robert, a boy who was working with him, to pass him a pipe. But Robert was slow to respond.

"Did you hear me, boy? I said pass me that pipe," Fred ordered.

When Robert failed to respond a second time, Fred told him he was going to fire him if he didn't do what he said. By this time, a girl had passed by, and Robert finally handed Fred the pipe.

"I'm sorry, Mr. Fred," Robert said. "But you see, I split my breeches not too long ago while working. And that girl who just passed by? That was my girlfriend. If I had gotten the pipe for you right then, she would have seen my behind."

Chuckling to himself, Fred forgave the poor boy.

Others noted Fred's passion for the well-being of others, like the time he took two elderly brothers into his home. The men were in their seventies and had become senile. One was going blind and the other was just about deaf. The relative they were living with, who was taking care of them, had died, leaving them homeless. They had grown up with Fred, and he couldn't rest until he knew they were in good hands. When he couldn't find anyone to care for them, he and Ernestine took them in and cared for them until they passed away.

Then there was a time in January 1989, his first year as mayor, when a gas-line leak caused most of the town's residents to lose their heat. After the problem was fixed, Fred took it upon himself to visit the town's elderly and make sure the pilot light on their heaters was lit. When he entered their homes, most of the residents were wrapped from head to toe in quilts and blankets but still trembling from the extreme cold. After Fred had restored their heat, many of them cried and hugged him in relief. One time, as he was leaving the home of a white woman, she walked him to the door and, with grateful tears in her eyes, asked how much he charged. Fred looked at her face, and the tears running down her now reddening cheeks as she started to get warm from the heat, and replied, "There's no charge. I'm getting my pay right now."

The stories of his service to his community are many.

That evening, as Fred looked out across the audience, at both black and white faces, he thought about the time those white boys rode their ponies through his and his friends' marble game, and how he got so mad he threw a rock and hit one of them in the back of the head. Who would have thought that the grandchildren of those boys—the grandchildren of people who once called him nigger—would grow up to honor his life of service and address him as Mayor Montgomery?

Fred believes God vindicates for us, and that all we have to do "is give our problems to him." Now, much older and wiser, Fred gives his struggles to God. "If we could wait a few seconds, instead of immediately saying or doing something harsh to someone, then we'd probably be able to pass off whatever happened and move on," he said. "God wants us to be as patient with each other as he is with us."

As Fred's eyes continued to skim the audience that night, he was slightly disappointed that Rev. George Hart couldn't be there. He had telephoned to let Fred know he couldn't make it but promised to be there in spirit. Fred would have liked to have seen him at the ceremony. After all, he wouldn't have been mayor without Hart.

Fred had run into Hart about a year before he stepped down as mayor. He was paying a bill at the dentist's office when a bearded white man approached him and asked if he recognized him. The man looked familiar, but he wasn't sure. The man then said, "I was the one who pulled you out of the river, nearly thirty years ago." Fred moved a few steps closer, and sure enough, it was him. He didn't recognize him because of the hair on his face and the added weight. They both embraced and burst into tears. People in the waiting room who didn't even know what was going on became emotional just watching them.

Hart told him he was in town to see a friend and decided to visit the dentist for a quick checkup. Fred invited him to the house to see Ernestine. As they were leaving the office, they both glanced at the calendar on the receptionist's desk and came to an eerie realization: it was the same day as the boating accident—the day Hart saved Fred's life.

On their way home from the ceremony, with his son driving and Ernestine sitting next to him in the back seat, they passed the railroad tracks where Fred had attempted to take his life. He thought once again about Hart and how he had pulled him from the river. Then he looked into Ernestine's beautiful eyes, saw his son in the front driving, watched as the white people waved at him as he passed by, and prayed: "God, how merciful you are. Thank you for sparing me."

With tears in his eyes, Fred remembered what his grandmother Callie had once told him when he was little: "There's going to be a better day." *She was right*, Fred thought. *And it felt good to be alive.*

Since stepping down as mayor, Fred continues to be the curator and main tour guide at the Alex Haley Museum, sharing his stories and those of Alex like a faithful servant guided by a quiet voice from on high. Every year, people come to the museum from around the world, some by the busload. Children who don't like school or aren't making the grades are motivated to do better when they hear about their childhood experiences. Countless adults are inspired by their triumph over adversity and often make return visits with others. Fred constantly receives letters from people who have visited the museum or read about him or Alex.

One woman from Bristol, Virginia, saw a story about Fred

that I had written for the Associated Press in her local newspaper and wrote him a letter:

> I'm sixty and have been in my small town since I was four. When I was in school I couldn't understand why all of us, white and black, couldn't eat, drink, and go to school together. This wasn't right. But through God's grace, hopefully we'll continue to improve. By the way, I'm white, but what difference does it make? God made us *all*.[3]

I'm among those repeat visitors. Every time I visit home, I make time to see my old friend. And, at thirty-three, I'm still following and absorbing his wisdom. Sometimes I stay overnight with him and Ernestine at their place. "Only two writers have slept in that bed you're in, and that's you and Alex," Fred told me one night. "He stayed in this guest bedroom every time he came to see me. He was welcome, and so are you."

I can't help but think back to that first time I met Fred. He gave me a tour of the museum, then took the time to sit and talk with me afterward. I was so impressed with not only the stories about Alex but his own life that I couldn't wait to tell others about him. Whenever I think about his miraculous existence, his undying love and faith, I'm reminded of the story of Corrie ten Boom, a Holocaust survivor.

During World War II, Corrie and her family risked their lives to help Jews escape the Nazis by hiding them in their home. The gestapo eventually raided the home, and Corrie and her family were arrested and sent to different concentration camps. Corrie and her sister, Betsie, were sent to Ravensbrück, one of the worst camps. However, they refused to succumb to the horrible conditions surrounding them. Corrie and Betsie read passages from a little Bible they had managed to smuggle into their barrack, lifting the spirits and increasing the faith of many other prisoners. Betsie died at the camp, but Corrie was released. She later learned that her release had been a mistake, and that about a week after she was let go, all the women her age at the camp were killed. She believed God had kept her alive for a reason. Corrie began a worldwide ministry, spanning more than sixty countries, telling everyone who would listen about what she and Betsie had experienced in Ravensbrück. Before her death at age ninety-one, she said: "There is no pit so deep that God's love is not deeper still."[4]

Fred was once in that pit, but God pulled him out. God will do the same for all of us. We just need to have faith. That's what I tell people when I talk about Fred Montgomery, and what God has done for him.

• • •

I truly believe that it was my faith and a new, forgiving mindset concerning white people I learned from Fred that helped me get through one of the more trying times in my life.

On Friday night, February 1, 2002, I was traveling down one of the streets leading out of the predominantly white suburb where I worked, when a police car put on its flashing lights behind me. The speed limit was forty miles per hour, and my speedometer showed I was going about thirty-five miles per hour. What was the problem? I pulled over and the cop, a white man who appeared to be in his early to mid-forties, approached my window. He said he'd pulled me over because my left taillight was out and just wanted to warn me. However, he proceeded to check my license. He was taking a long time, and I started to get a little nervous. When he returned, he asked me to get out and face the vehicle. It was then that he put my hands behind my back and started to handcuff me. He said a green capias appeared when he checked my license, meaning an order had been issued for my arrest. When I asked him what for, he said he didn't know, but that I'd find out once I got to the police station downtown. He seemed a bit puzzled that such an order had been issued even though I had a valid driver's license.

I couldn't believe it was happening. I'd seen people handcuffed and pushed headfirst into police cars on television, but I never thought it would happen to me. What would be in store for me when I got to the precinct? What would people say when they found out I'd been arrested? I was worried, but then I took a deep breath, exhaled slowly, and told myself, *Everything is going to be all right. God will see to it.*

When I got to the station, I learned the green capias had been issued on me because I had failed to appear in court. At first, I thought it was a mistake. Then I remembered that several months earlier my license had been suspended because of several unpaid speeding tickets. I had paid the tickets and gotten a new license but failed to appear before the judge to show proof that I did so. That was my fault, and I paid the penalty: two days in jail without bond.

I was placed in a holding cell that was only about ten feet by twelve feet with ten other guys, mostly black and Hispanic, except for one white guy. There was little room to be comfortable. The cell also reeked of urine, with a toilet that looked as though it hadn't been cleaned in weeks, if ever. I sat there for about three hours before they moved me to another, less-crowded cell with a guy who also missed a court date. He was a short, dumpy, unshaven white man by the name of John Tango. It was his second time in.

John said he had just gotten a job as a construction foreman and was afraid his arrest might jeopardize his position. I hadn't given it a lot of thought, but I realized my job might also be in jeopardy. My bosses had always been pretty down-to-earth and understanding. But two days in jail? When I told John it was my first time in, he gave me some advice: "Mind your own business, and you'll be okay." Of course, it wasn't anything I didn't already know, but I appreciated him telling me anyway. After waiting for several more hours, John and I were given the continental breakfast: bologna, light bread, cold grits, and warm juice. By this time I was starving, so I ate it—all of it.

I was moved around about two more times before a nurse drew my blood. Then I was taken to a larger area with steel benches in the center and cells lining the walls. Most of the cells were already full, so new guys like me were given floor mats and placed wherever there was room. I was sent to one with two white men. One claimed to be Willie Nelson's cousin and told me to call him Cousin Willie. The other guy, who went by Bob, was a recovering alcoholic waiting to go before a judge for allegedly abusing his wife.

Cousin Willie, a skinny, bearded dude who coughed profusely, was a cocaine addict. He said he'd been a big-time country singer in Nashville at one time and had made a lot of money. But he lost all of it because of his addiction and now lived on the streets. I found out that a lot of the inmates were homeless, and they saw jail as a refuge, like the Salvation Army. After all, they were fed three times a day and had a place to sleep out of the elements. I relaxed as best I could on the floor mat, with my feet at the base of another grimy toilet and my head near the cell's door, while Cousin Willie and Bob slept in the bunk beds. Ironically, two men of the race I once hated were now my roommates.

Around six in the morning, I officially became an inmate at the Davidson County Jail. I was taken to the second floor where I signed a few forms, removed my clothes, showered, and then put on a bright orange jumpsuit with orange slip-on shoes trimmed in white. I was given a small rectangular crate that contained some basic necessities—soap, toothbrush, toilet paper, underwear, T-shirts, blanket—and then moved to the building gymnasium with about thirty other inmates. There, each of us was given a plastic cot that resembled a small boat and a floor mat to put it on.

The temperature outside was probably about forty-five degrees, but it had to have been about forty in that gym. We all complained, especially after two inmates had seizures as a result of the cold. But the security officer said there was something wrong with the heating system and we'd just have to make do. We were given extra wool blankets, which felt like sleeping under a large S.O.S soap pad. Nevertheless, I made do. That gym was going to be my home until Monday morning.

Doing nothing was probably the toughest part for me. Even though I was there for only two days, it seemed like forever. I couldn't fathom staying there for months or years. But people were doing it, right there with me and elsewhere. I thought about my cousin Harold. In a weird sort of way, I kind of admired him. He told me in his letters that the key to surviving behind bars was being mentally tough. I now understood what he meant. To help pass the time, I talked with the other inmates. They reminded me of the guys from my old stomping ground—those who had the potential to make it out of the hood but never did because somewhere life threw them a curveball.

One guy, who was there on a drug charge, as many were, managed to fix a malfunctioning phone in the gym by meticulously connecting certain wires, letting us make calls. This guy could have been an electrical engineer. Then there was another guy who talked about past presidents and how they compared to the current one. He talked confidently about various administrations as if he were getting the information directly from a book. He could have been a politician or a history professor, but instead he ended up a convicted felon serving time for burglary.

They reminded me of Sammy the Pimp and West Indian Archie in Alex Haley's *The Autobiography of Malcolm X*. Sammy was organized and could easily have been some type of a businessman outside the pimp game and peddling reefer. West Indian Archie ran numbers and would have made a good accountant. But somewhere in their lives they got caught up in their environment and, with no strong influence to lead them to do what was right, resorted to lives of crime to survive. The guys I saw in that county jail were no different.

On Monday, around 10:00 a.m., the security officer walked into the gym and called my name. As I gathered my blankets to turn them in, John asked if I would contact his brother for him. The day before, John, who suffered from high blood pressure, had to be rushed to the hospital for stabilization. He thought his lawyer should know about it, but he was having trouble contacting him and wanted his brother to try. I told him I would help him, and we shook hands. During our many conversations, I told him my profession. As I was leaving, he quipped, "I'm sure you'll write about this someday."

I smiled.

After my arrest, Jacques, a good friend, had retrieved my car so it wouldn't get towed and had called the bureau early Saturday to tell them what had happened. When I got home, I contacted my editor to provide the details. To my relief, she understood and was sympathetic. I then called John's brother. He was glad to know that John was all right and said he would contact the lawyer. It felt good to help John.

A few months later, I told a black policeman who'd become a good friend of mine and a supervisor in the Davidson County Criminal Court clerk's office what happened to me. Both agreed that because I had a valid driver's license, when I was pulled over by the officer, I shouldn't have been taken to jail. Even though I didn't show up to court and so had been issued a green capias, it should have been cleared up at the police station. They said I had a possible case and wouldn't blame me if I contacted a lawyer. But I didn't think any vindication was necessary, because I believe God allowed the incident to happen for a reason.

After seeing those men in jail and pondering how different their lives could have been with more positive intervention during childhood, I decided to work at a group home for troubled teens called Youth Emergency Services of Middle Tennessee. By sharing some of my experiences and telling them about the men in my family who overcame adversity, I hoped to provide the kids with the fortitude to stay on the straight and narrow path. I also wanted them to see the consequences of straying. So I orchestrated a trip to the Riverbend Maximum Security Institution in Nashville, a home to some of the most ruthless criminals. While there, the kids heard from a robust inmate named Ben, who was serving a life sentence for murder.

"It's not the big things that I miss, but the little things," Ben told them. "What I wouldn't give to sleep in my own bed, to push a shopping cart in a grocery store and pick out the food I want. But I lost my freedom. I'm told not only what to eat, but when to go to sleep, and when to get up. Straighten up, boys. You don't want to come in here."

What Ben said that day didn't just rattle those kids. I, too, was touched by the truth of his words. As we walked out the prison gates, passing the razor-wire fence towering on either side, I realized Ben and many others wouldn't see freedom for years, if ever. A lot of times, we take our freedom for granted.

Later on, I thought about the day I was released from the Davidson County Jail, and how comfortable it felt to sleep in my own bed again and eat the food I wanted. I was thankful to God for his mercy, for sparing me from what could easily have been my life. That first weekend in February 2002, at the county jail, I saw what might have happened if I had smoked with my cousins years ago.

I saw robbers and addicts.

I saw me.

CHAPTER 12

THE GOOD

Find the good and praise it.
—**ALEX HALEY**

Years have passed since I first met Fred Montgomery. I must admit I'm still mystified when I think about how our paths crossed and how I came to write about his life. Was it fate? Did some of the things that happened in my life lead to our meeting?

I dodged a life of substance abuse and crime. I wanted to be a pilot but ended up a writer. My grandmother always told me, "God is going to use you for something." Then there was Maya Angelou, who wrote back saying she believed I'd "do something marvelous." Well, I don't know about all that. But I do know I'm a better person because of Fred. His life gave me a credible blueprint on how to deal with life's problems—and even grow stronger because of them. As I listened to Fred and his words of wisdom, I noticed some things I'd heard before but for whatever reason had forgotten.

If we're fortunate, God will send someone our way to remind us of how he wants us to live. In many cases, that person will be wiser and much older, like our elders. Someone who's been refined by life's trials and tribulations, instead of tarnished by them. Throughout all of life's struggles and tragedies, Fred managed to find love, courage, forgiveness, and faithfulness. But most of all, he firmly embraced the latter, like a modern-day Job.

I remember Fred telling me that when he was in his fifties, a doctor had discovered blood in his urine. That night, instead of becoming flustered, he got down on his knees and asked God to "fix whatever is wrong." After he got up, he had a strange urge to go into the kitchen and drink two glasses of water. Then, a few days later, the doctor couldn't find a trace of blood.

The more Fred told me about such experiences and other adversities he'd overcome, the more I understood why Alex Haley wanted to write a book about him. According to Fred, Alex often said, "Find the good and praise it." Alex definitely found the good in Fred. As did I. But I saw an even deeper meaning to Alex's statement when I came across Galatians 5:22–23: "But the fruit of the Spirit is love, joy, peace, forbearance, kindness, goodness, faithfulness, gentleness and self-control. Against such things there is no law."

When we search for the good, we are actually seeking the fruit of the Spirit—a relationship with God, a friendship. This is the spiritual bond Fred, my father, his father, and the other men in my family had with God that allowed them to know whom to call on in their times of need when no one else seemed to be of help to them. Now I, too, have that relationship with God. However, like most men, I used to be stubborn and thought I could do life on my own.

I became distracted during college and prayed less and less. It was hard for me to kneel and talk to someone I couldn't see. But thanks to Fred and the miracles he shared with me, I have a strong faith. I pray and read my Bible more often. Things have happened in my life—positive things—that taught me to be more compassionate. I no longer feel hatred toward whites or boil over with anger when things don't work out. But most of all, I have become more forgiving.

The bitterness I once harbored over my father's broken promises and the times we have lost because of his alcoholism has been replaced with the joy of having him in my life clean and sober. We now spend more time together. I even convinced him to do something I thought he'd never do with me: go to the movies. My father very rarely went to the movies. Whenever he came to visit me and I offered to treat him to the latest feature, he always turned me down. However, on January 25, 2003, that all changed. My sisters and I were visiting our parents that day, and we decided to go see the *Antwone Fisher* story. When I asked our father if he wanted to join us and Mom, he said no. But when I went to his bedroom to tell him we were leaving, there he sat with his coat and hat. I asked where he was going, and he replied, "With you." That was the first movie my father, at sixty-eight years old, had gone out to see in nearly thirty years. And he enjoyed it. We all did. As a family.

Now that my father is fully back in my life, I don't hesitate to say "I love you" or tell him how much I appreciate him. I realize how fortunate I am, being that many young men I know are fatherless. I also have a better sense of who I am, giving me a feeling of completeness that encompasses confidence and responsibility. Who knows? I may finally be ready for that special person.

At the time this book was completed in 2002, Fred and Ernestine had been married sixty-seven years. My father's parents were married sixty-three years before my grandfather Daddy Roy died. Fred told me that prayer and communication were keys to their relationship's longevity. My grandfather told me the same. One day, I watched as Fred and Ernestine interacted with each other. They laughed and talked, enjoying the simplicity of each other's presence. Later that evening, Fred told me another reason for their marital success: seeing the inner beauty.

"Ernestine and I are old and wrinkled. I mean look at her over there. She can hardly get out of that chair," he said with a slight chuckle. "But when I look at her, she's as beautiful as when we first met. You know why? I'm looking on the inside."

That's what I didn't do with the woman to whom I was once engaged. I was engrossed with her attractiveness. But if I had taken the time to look beyond her beauty, I would have seen that we were incompatible and saved us both a lot of heartache. I talked with several young men who had similar experiences. They all said that once they let go of their egos, humbled themselves, and began to pray for direction, they found their mates for life. And if infidelity reared its ugly head, they knew to whom they should turn and ask to help squash it.

The mate God chooses for you will play a role in your spiritual well-being. A person not of the same yoke, who is argumentative and causes constant tension, might drive one to sin. Fred shared with me 2 Corinthians 6:14: "Do not be yoked together with unbelievers. For what do righteousness and wickedness have in common? Or what fellowship can light have with darkness?" If one day I'm blessed to have a son, and he should ask me what type of woman he should marry, I want to be able to say without hesitation, "Someone like your mother."

Indeed, I'm wiser now when it comes to finding my significant other. But back then, because of the increasingly violent world in which we lived, I found myself going back and forth on the issue of marriage and children. At one point, I decided I didn't want to be a father. There were several factors that caused me to feel that way. One was the death of seven-year-old Jake Joyner, a little boy who was getting his hair cut in my cousin's barbershop when he was fatally shot during a botched robbery. Shortly after that, it was the Oklahoma City bombing, in which many innocent children lost their lives. Then came the terrorist attacks on September 11, 2001, which killed thousands and left just as many little boys and girls without a mother or a father to tuck them in at night. In an email to all Associated Press employees concerning 9/11, company president Lou Boccardi wrote, "These are difficult and dangerous days."

As I had done so many times before, I went to Fred like a child seeking consolation from an older loved one. His wisdom once again comforted me, and he helped me to see the good. He reminded me of the Middle Passage, and how one out of every four slaves on those ships died. He said they also risked death almost every day on plantations in the new land. But still, many remained prayerful and hopeful. Even though their lives were threatened, those faithful didn't stop having babies. They just put their trust in God and gave their children as much love as possible until their deaths, whenever that might be.

We live in an unfair world. But just because a life is taken away doesn't mean we should stop creating it. Sadly, there will be more terrorist attacks and wars, as well as kidnappings, murders, and other terrible acts in our very communities. Those who do evil want to disrupt our lives. However, their attempts are foiled when we pick ourselves up and move on. God has reasons for everything, reasons our finite minds can't understand. For instance, why did he let thousands die in the terrorist attacks of 9/11, yet spare the lives of nine miners in Somerset County, Pennsylvania, who were trapped at least 250 feet underground for more than three days? There is no sure answer. But there were definite outcomes. The attacks united America and caused those who didn't believe in God or had lost faith to flock to their nearest churches to seek his mercy and salvation. Thousands lost their lives, but millions were saved. A Michigan man probably said it best in the aftermath: "Although some lives are taken, and some are rescued, the Lord's in control of all things for good."

This goodness was made plain to me as I watched one of the events held around the nation to commemorate the first-year anniversary of the 9/11 attacks. I saw our indisputable commonality. At Ground Zero in New York City, where the World Trade Center once stood, families and friends of all races—blacks, whites, Hispanics, Asians, and other races—gathered together to remember those they lost. There was no hatred, no racism, just tears of sorrow all flowing into a melting pot of grief. Like the ocean that's the same color as far as the eye can see, those people were also the same—on the inside.

Fred's stories about his hatred toward whites and the events that took place to change the way he felt were medicine for my soul. I thought long and hard about his realization that not all whites hated blacks, and that many of them were loving and caring people. Additionally, he knew that those who may once have had hatred in their hearts could change. For instance, Fred later learned from Mrs. Agnes Pipkin that it was Sam Thum who recommended him to the family to work in their store. "Fred is good help, and honest," Thum told them.

After learning what Thum had said, Fred thought about that time he helped him change the disc on the plow. It was apparent that no matter how mean or ornery a person may be, God has planted a seed of good in each of us. But to make the seed grow, we must water it with his love—and thus change our hearts.

Fred also shared the story of one white man who allowed God to come into his life, inspiring him to write a song for the ages. John Newton had lived a life at sea since age eleven. His mother prayed for him to be a minister, teaching him the Scriptures at an early age, but Newton desired to be a sailor like his father. He grew up to become one of the most ruthless sailors, and slave-trading was his specialty.

On one particular voyage, Newton's ship was caught in a fierce storm. It ripped the vessel's canvas sails and splintered the wood on one side of the ship. It seemed he was doomed. While fearing for his life, Newton remembered his mother's prayers and the scriptures she taught him; so in desperation, he called out, "Lord, have mercy upon us." God spared his life and those of his crew that day. Humbled by the experience, he reflected on God's mercy, and wrote: "Thro' many dangers, toils and snares, I have already come; 'tis grace has bro't me safe thus far, and grace will lead me home." These words would become part of the beloved song Newton would later pen: "Amazing Grace."

After his deliverance, Newton fulfilled his mother's wish and became a minister. He got out of the slave trade and preached heavily against slavery. As a matter of fact, his thoughts were very influential in securing the British abolition. Up until his death, at the age of eighty-two, Newton never ceased to be amazed by the transforming power of God's grace. He told his friends before he died, "My memory is nearly gone, but I remember two things: that I am a great sinner, and that Christ is a great Savior."[5]

In my dealings with white people, I had let my sinful nature get the best of me. But Fred's faith in God's grace made me look in the mirror and accept what I had been doing. In a sense, I was no better than the racist whites who marginalize blacks and other minorities. I perpetuated the same type of ideology by lumping all the whites under the category of "haters." Fred changed that.

I began to look for the good stories about whites, such as the one concerning Maryland linebacker Randy Earle, who was born a crack baby. The family of one of his white teammates and other residents in Farmingdale, New York, helped raise him after his mother and father—both intravenous drug users—died of AIDS, which also claimed the lives of his little brother and sister. I also reflected on the white people in my own life. Those who had assisted or influenced me in some way over the course of my life, such as Carlie Ann Davis, my fifth-grade teacher, who encouraged me to read and realize I had the ability to become whatever and go wherever those books described.

There were others in high school and college, such as my feature-writing instructor, Dr. Glenn Himebaugh. He helped hone my writing skills even more, which allowed me to get several internships and eventually gain the attention of Kent Flanagan, the Associated Press bureau chief in Nashville, who hired me right out of college. I didn't have a lot of experience, but Kent saw something in me and gave me a chance. There was Joe Edwards, my colleague at the AP, who told me about a national tourism magazine that was looking for someone to do a feature story on the Alex Haley Museum. He was key to my even meeting Fred. And then there was the caring letter Judge Pugh sent me concerning my cousin Anderson. If my initial feelings toward whites hadn't been so saturated with hatred, I probably would have taken to heart one of the most profound statements ever made to me by a white person.

It was 1992, and Bill Clinton, who had won the Democratic nomination, selected Al Gore from Carthage, Tennessee, to be his running mate. My assignment was to go to Carthage and get reactions from the townsfolk. I went with a white coworker named Mark, an AP photographer. One of the people I talked to was Gore's second-grade teacher, Eleanor Smotherman. She was close to ninety, but I was amazed by her sharp mind. She was also very kind and gentle. After the interview, I realized there was something I needed to clarify, so I called her back about an hour later. When she answered, I told her my name and then said jokingly, in case she'd forgotten, that "I was the dark-skinned one." Her response was unexpected: "Young man, it doesn't matter what color you are, it's what you have upstairs." I didn't really expect her to say anything, let alone that. I realized I had already judged her. Because of her age and the fact that she lived in a rural town, I assumed she was one of those whites who refused to divorce segregation and remained married to Jim Crow. But Ms. Smotherman was different; she was open-minded.

When I look back, I realize all those white people were placed in my life for a reason. I remember the lesson Fred said he learned after Rev. George Hart pulled him from the freezing river. He said, "Whoever God chooses to send his blessing by, receive it regardless of what color the messenger is, and be thankful for it." From Ms. Smotherman, I learned another lesson: the age of the messenger doesn't matter either.

On one of my visits to the Alex Haley Museum, I brought a special person with me for Fred to inspire. That person would also play a part in my getting rid of years of guilt.

I was touched by Fred's desire to help others, in particular, the two elderly men he took into his home and cared for until they died. I felt it was time for me to reach out as well. So I got in contact with Harold's son, Devin. Harold had started calling me at least once a month from prison and told me Devin was a sharp young man. But I didn't know just how put together he was until I talked with him. And when I saw him, his resemblance to his father—the eyes, the nose, the way he walked—was striking. Despite having to help his grandmother take care of his now seven younger siblings, the seventeen-year-old had made the honor roll several times, was a leader in his ROTC class, and somehow found time to write poetry. I thought Devin might get some ideas for his poetry from hearing Fred's stories. But even more, I believed this wise old man was just somebody a young man should know.

When we got to the museum, Fred took him on a tour.

Watching Devin hang on Fred's every word and seeing his eyes widen as he looked around the museum made me think about the images that had stayed with me: the griot and the boy standing behind him, cast members like James Earl Jones, Binter Kinte's piercing eyes, Alex Haley looking out over the ocean from a dock in Annapolis, Maryland.

At the end of the tour, Devin walked up to me and said, "Thank you," with a big smile on his face. He said Fred had inspired him and that he now had a lot to write about. His enlightenment was evident in the words of a poem he wrote:

> Who am I? That's the question I would ask when I looked in the mirror. Some days he looked as though his world was falling apart. . . . Then he remembered the words of an old wise man. . . . Ancestors determined to push forward, to become doctors, lawyers, teachers, writers, mayors. Now I know the person in the mirror. He's been inside all along, a fighter. He's a reflection of those who paved the way before him. Because of them, I am.

I beamed at Devin's newfound enthusiasm. His words and the expression on his face let me know he was going to be all right. Suddenly, my years of guilt seemed to disappear. I was atoning for the time I sat and did nothing while his father got high. I could clearly see Devin was heading in the right direction, and I was going to be there to make sure he stayed the course. This time I was going to do something— something good.

That evening, I left Fred and Devin alone and walked around to the front of the museum where Alex is buried. On his headstone is a list of his published and unpublished works. At the bottom is Fred Montgomery. I thought about those interviews Alex had with his old buddy, and his strong desire to tell the world about Fred's life, his faith, his love. Now, years later, his story is being told.

As I stood there over the grave of the great storyteller, a feeling of gratefulness, of completeness, consumed me. At that moment, I envisioned myself walking down that dock, tapping Alex on the shoulder, and telling him: "Here it is. The book about your boyhood friend. The one who touched your life and mine. Now, through this book, his life will enrich the lives of many. You don't have to look any further."

I found him. The griot of Henning.

AFTERWORD

And we know that in all things God works for
the good of those who love him, who have
been called according to his purpose.

—ROMANS 8:28

O n July 12, 2006, my good friend and mentor Fred
Montgomery passed away at age eighty-nine. I spoke at his
funeral in Henning, Tennessee, which was attended by local
and national dignitaries. I was a little nervous at first, because
I wasn't used to speaking in front of a crowd of people. But I
took a deep breath and the words came freely.

"Alex Haley would often say, 'find the good and praise it.' I
found it in a jewel, an old, wise man tucked away in Henning."

After the funeral service, a feeling came over me, similar
to one I had ten years earlier when I left Fred after meeting
him for the first time at the Alex Haley Museum. I remember

wanting to tell everyone I encountered about him. To impart the wisdom he had given me. To share his goodness. Now, that feeling was stronger than ever. Little did I know I would have numerous opportunities to talk about this West Tennessee griot and continue his legacy. One of the more memorable occasions took place in fall 2008 in Chicago.

Lillian Frazier, an administrator at St. Ethelreda School, one of the largest African American elementary schools in the Chicago Archdiocese, contacted me at the Associated Press after purchasing *Finding the Good* at a local bookstore. When we talked, she asked what it would take for me to come to Chicago and speak to a group of sixth, seventh, and eighth graders about the book. Not having any idea what was really in store for me, I told her it would take the coverage for my flight and a $500 honorarium.

The day of the event, a limousine picked me up at my hotel. At the school, there was a red carpet—yes, the real deal—and students lining both sides as I walked up the stairs. "Welcome, Mr. Johnson!" they shouted.

I learned that the school had ordered the book for their students and had incorporated some of its themes of forgiveness, unity, and hope into their classroom curriculums. At the end of my discussion, students lined up in front of mics to ask questions. They were so engaged I was amazed. I could tell by their questions that the book, that Fred, had made a lasting impression. But what happened as I was about to leave nearly floored me.

The school's principal, Dr. Denise Spells, handed me an

envelope and thanked me for coming. When I opened it, there was a check for $2,000. Dumbfounded, I turned to Dr. Spells and told her, "I only asked for $500."

She smiled, then said, "We found the good."

There's more. About a month later, I received a package in the mail from the school. Inside were close to seventy letters from students expressing how the book had affected their lives. One seventh grader wrote:

> Dear Mr. Johnson, your book is still in our hearts. Almost every day Mrs. Spells tells us to "find the good" in every situation. I didn't notice before, but ever since I have read your book, I have prayed every day, and now I'm not in many bad situations because I am talking to God about it. I will continue to find the good in everyone.

She ended her letter with this scripture: "Whoever seeks good finds favor, but evil comes to one who searches for it" (Prov. 11:27).

An eighth grader wrote:

> By reading your book I found out a lot of things to cherish. For example, when Fred wanted to kill himself, God didn't let him. That tells me that God is real, and he only wants the best for us. I have had personal experiences in my life when I just wanted to die, but God held me close and he didn't let go. Your book helped me to realize that there is some good in every situation, we just have to find it.

Mrs. Spells' son, Shakir, was enrolled at St. Ethelreda and was among the students who sent me a letter. "Your book changed my life forever," the fourteen-year-old wrote. I was able to contact Shakir in December 2020 through his mother, who was still the school's principal. The now twenty-six-year-old said his mother would always tell him to "find the good in every situation," and he's strived to do so every day, even during undoubtedly one of the most difficult times of his life.

"My first year in college, my dad died, and I really didn't want to go back to school," said Shakir, who was attending Iowa State University. "But I found the good in the situation in that [my dad] wanted me to go to school. He brought me here for my orientation. That was the good that I felt. And I needed to keep pushing through, to get done with school, and continue on with my goals."

And he's done just that. Shakir graduated from Iowa State with a bachelor's degree in kinesiology and health, and at the time of writing this afterword, he has one year left in a program to become a registered nurse. He said the principles of *Finding the Good* helped him care for his patients, particularly during the coronavirus pandemic. "There were bad situations," said Shakir. "But every day, I seemed to find a positive outcome. Something from a patient or a staff member that helped me get through."

In early 2020, I found myself struggling to find the good in an unprecedented year. Of course, no one can predict the future. But I don't think anybody expected 2020 to turn out the way it did. It was mentally, physically, and emotionally exhausting.

The coronavirus pandemic that began in early spring claimed the lives of millions of people and revealed even more the gaping disparity in health care for underserved communities. Then that summer, the brutal, public death of a black man (George Floyd) at the hands of a police officer in Minneapolis, Minnesota, led to an explosion of racial unrest that had been shimmering from a string of other African American deaths at the hands of law enforcement. Add to all that probably one of the most polarizing presidential elections the nation has ever seen, and it all seemed just too much to bear.

But then, prayerfully, I started looking for the good. And I found the inspiring stories of health-care workers and first responders—as well as everyday people—who risked their lives to help others. I saw people who had once ignored the reality of racism remove their blinders, embrace humanity, and work alongside non-whites to create change. I saw hope for a truly united nation. However, it was an unexpected phone call I received that helped me to really envision what America could be.

Rev. George Hart, the man who saved Fred and Charles Halliburton in the boating accident, contacted me amid the worldwide protests that had erupted following the death of George Floyd. The last time we had spoken was when I was working on *Finding the Good*, nearly twenty years earlier. He said the racial tension and divisiveness made him think about the book, and that if there was ever a time for its message, it was now. The seventy-eight-year-old then shared a personal story about an incident that happened in Memphis, Tennessee, in 1968, three days after the death of Martin Luther King Jr. It was almost as if he wanted to unburden himself.

At the time, Hart said he was a salesman in the wholesale liquor business. He had left a sales meeting and was visiting some of his customers in a rough neighborhood in southeast Memphis, who had been victims of the rioting and looting in the wake of Dr. King's death. While in the neighborhood, Hart ran into a group of black men who appeared to be in their twenties. There were about ten of them, and they made it clear they didn't want him in their neighborhood. He was afraid, but for some reason, he believed he would be okay if he was honest and sincere with the men. So he listened to what they had to say.

"They told me they did not want me in their neighborhood, because it was their neighborhood," said Hart. "They said they had not been treated right for a long time, and I agreed with them. I told them my customers had not been treated right also, because their stores had been looted and some of them destroyed. I let them know I was going to spend the rest of my life trying to help people get along with one another."

He left the neighborhood unharmed. Earlier, his boss had suggested he carry a weapon when going into certain neighborhoods. But Hart objected because he didn't like guns. "I'm so glad I didn't have one that day. Because I might have used it," he said.

After the incident, Hart went straight to the bishop of the Episcopal Church he was attending and told him about his encounter and that he meant what he told those men. The bishop asked him if he'd ever considered attending a seminary. Hart's faith had been growing over the years, and he saw the encounter as a sign. So he told the bishop he was interested, and he helped Hart get the money he needed to attend seminary. "I went, was eventually ordained, and served in the priesthood for thirty-five years," said Hart.

What he learned in the seminary along with his personal desire to help others motivated him to act that fateful winter day in 1978. When we talked, he shared something new about the boating accident.

He said he and his hunting companion were in their boat looking for geese when off in the distance they spotted what looked like several orange life jackets in the water. As they got closer, they realized they weren't just life jackets. "We didn't see black people in the river, we didn't see white people in the river," recalled Hart. "We saw God's children in dire straits. And we were there to help."

Hart was not the only person who had mentioned the relevancy of *Finding the Good* nearly two decades since it was first published. So I got to thinking: What if the book was republished with a section added to update the readers on what has happened since? I approached the publisher of Nelson Books with the idea, and he agreed to publish a revised edition.

As I reflected on what I should include in this afterword, one story that stood out above all is that of my cousin Harold, who was released from prison in June 2007 after serving nearly ten years. In *Finding the Good*, I wrote about the guilt that stayed with me for many years because I felt responsible for the path he took. When Harold was released, I was there to greet him. I wrote about that day in an editorial in the *Tennessean*:

> I had waited almost a decade—9 years and 11 months to be exact. So, I didn't mind taking off from my job in Nashville and driving three hours to pick up my cousin Harold from the Northwest Correctional Complex in Tiptonville [Tennessee]. As we drove away from the complex, I watched in my rearview mirror as it faded into the distance. I couldn't help but smile. My guilt was fading with it.[6]

Since his release, Harold has not looked back. He works diligently alongside his father at their successful upholstery business in Memphis and goes home to his sweet wife, Helen. They married in December 2016, six months after I wed my lovely life partner, Alicia. Harold's father served as his best man.

Their father-and-son story is part of a screenplay that was adapted from *Finding the Good*. The screenplay came about after Karla Winfrey, an Emmy Award–winning producer and documentarian, visited the Alex Haley Museum (now Alex Haley Museum and Interpretive Center) and was given a tour by Fred Montgomery. She was so moved by the stories of Fred and Haley that she has made it her mission to turn his life into a feature film. And she still continues to garner support for the project. One advocate is Hollywood screenwriter Antwone

Fisher, whom I had the privilege to sit and chat with during a visit to Los Angeles.

"It is rare that a project garners my attention like the Fred Montgomery story," Fisher wrote in a letter of support. "This moving story about the forgiving heart of an African American small-town mayor would touch the lives of many globally."

Since the time I got to know Fred Montgomery years ago, that has been my mission, my purpose. To share the story of his incredible life. It is a story that truly exemplifies, as the Scriptures state, no matter the situation, "in all things God works for the good of those who love him."

And that goodness is in all of us and around us. We just have to be willing to find it.

ACKNOWLEDGMENTS

Not one word of this book could have been written without God's guidance. Each day, before my fingers touched the keyboard, I prayed for wisdom and perseverance. Thank you for answering my prayer.

I want to thank my family for all their support, especially my two sisters—Cathy and Stephanie—for listening patiently as I read excerpts of the book over the phone. My maternal grandmother and my parents, who were alive when this book first published, have since passed on. But they remain alive on the pages of *Finding the Good* and in my heart. The prayers of my mother and grandmother are still blessing me.

Enormous thanks to Terrie Williams for helping me put this story in the right hands. And to Erma Byrd, Rhonda Crayton, Cedric Dent, Gail Hamilton, Steven Norman III, Phil Petrie, Howard and Beverly Robertson, Karla Winfrey, Burnice Winfrey, Adrienne Ingrum, Judi Durand, Julie Fairchild, Leroy Bobbitt, Michael Polite, and Sharon Presley for their support and always welcome advice. Thank you also to US senator Lamar Alexander for sharing your personal stories of Fred Montgomery and Alex Haley in the foreword. And, of course, thank you to my wife, Alicia, for your advice and loving support. You are absolutely wonderful.

I am also grateful to my first agent, Joann Davis; editor, Geoff Stone; and the rest of the Rutledge Hill family. And a special thank you to the publisher of Nelson Books, Timothy Paulson, and his amazing editorial team (Sujin Hong, you rock!) for republishing *Finding the Good* and making it even better. Thank you, Greg Johnson, my current agent, for helping to make that happen.

I am very appreciative to members of my blood family whose lives I discuss in the book in some capacity. You are inspirations, and I know what I've said about you will touch the lives of others.

Thanks to my colleagues at the Associated Press and others in the field of journalism, especially the late Ben Johnson and Peggy Peterman, whose guidance over the years helped me become a better writer. And I'm extremely grateful to Carlton, Lawrence, Luther, Jacques, Michael, Robbie, and my cousin Tony, who helped a brother when he needed it most. To you all, I say, "A-Phi!"

But most of all, thank you, Fred Montgomery, for allowing me to tell your story. Thank you for having faith in me. Thank you for *finding the good* in me.

As for the great storyteller Alex Haley, thanks for providing the *roots* from which I was able to grow.

May you both rest in peace.

APPENDIX

"Crack in the Family"

Essence, August 1992[7]

I knew my cousin Anderson pretty well when I was growing up. Because I have no brothers, he was like my big brother, and I always wanted to do everything he did and go everywhere he went.

I would watch him and his friends when they got together. They would sit around, shoot the breeze, smoke some marijuana. To me, it seemed harmless. But I never tried it, nor would my cousin let me.

I always asked him why he smoked it. He would simply say that it made him feel good, and then, ironically, he would threaten me: "If I ever catch you smoking marijuana, I'll kill you." Then he would take another long drag of a marijuana cigarette. Later the marijuana gave way to crack cocaine.

Anderson chose drugs as a momentary escape from the ghetto. He saw young men dying from cold-blooded shootings, overdoses and fights in the streets. I saw young men going to college and aspiring to become doctors and lawyers.

I felt like an Army dropout telling a Vietnam hero he didn't win the war. After all, what could I say? My cousin was fighting a war I knew nothing about, and he was losing.

At one point, Anderson actually enlisted in the Army for four years, and his life took a brief change for the better. I rejoiced. His return home was even more glorious. He looked like a new man when he arrived at the airport. His sister and I were elated.

Everything was fantastic for about a year. Then the entire environmental picture was redrawn—hanging out on the corner with old buddies, smoking marijuana, drinking liquor. But marijuana was not enough. Anderson had to find what all his friends were talking about. He had to find that "white girl"—cocaine.

When he found her, the symptoms came one after the other, as if he were suffering from some consuming disease. Anderson started by using half of his paycheck to buy rocks (crack, a solidified form of cocaine). Then he started spending his entire check. And when the money ran out, he pawned whatever he could get his hands on, even his mother's brass lamps.

I returned home from college to find a stranger. Anderson wasn't the same person I had seen only a year before. He had lost weight, his color was darker, and he sounded insincere and hopeless. What could I say to him? He was 30 years old; I was a 19-year-old college student.

But my heart was filled with love, and my hand reached out, for this was the man I had adopted as my brother. I knew the old Anderson, and I wanted him back. I asked him to quit drugs. He promised he would.

Prayers and words of caution, however, mean nothing to a man consumed in his own smoke-filled world. Anderson was arrested, finally, for stealing.

But my family's love runs deep. Anderson was bailed out of jail and placed in a veterans' rehabilitation center. Although he spent several months in counseling, a week after his release he was back on the streets, doing the same old thing. This time his only brother reached out and took my cousin into his home, only to have his hand slapped. Anderson robbed him.

Yet his brother did not put him out. He stuck by him even more. He knew Anderson was knocking on death's door. Fortunately, a higher being opened another door first. Anderson's brother was able to persuade him to attend church.

At first it was only through his family's urging that Anderson went to church. But after a while he started going every Sunday without a word being said to him. And every Sunday his mother's face glowed as he walked through the church door.

Now, thirty-four-year-old Anderson is celebrating more than a year of being drug-free and has a full-time job. He is attending church regularly, and he has assumed special roles in the church. In addition, he is actively playing a major role in helping others break their addiction to crack.

The last time I saw my cousin, I almost cried tears of joy. He was a fuller, livelier man—a man at whose courage I marveled. We talked for a long time. And before we finished, he said to me, "If I ever see you using crack, I'll kill you."

I laughed, joyously.

NOTES

1. Part of the speech is mentioned in Colin Campbell, "Republican Introducing Obama at Inauguration Quotes Alex Haley," *Observer*, January 21, 2013, http://observer.com/2013/01/republican-introducing-obama-at-inauguration-quotes-alex-haley.
2. Letter to author from Judge Ann Pugh on December 6, 1993.
3. Lucas L. Johnson, "Fred Montgomery: From Sharecropper to Mayor," Associated Press, September 13, 1999.
4. Corrie ten Boom, *The Hiding Place* (Grand Rapids, MI: Chosen Books, 1971), 8.
5. David B. Calhoun, "'Amazing Grace' John Newton and His Great Hymn," *Knowing & Doing* (Winter 2013): 5.
6. Lucas L. Johnson, "Free at Last: Escaping a Cycle of Drugs and Prison," *Tennessean*, October 29, 2017, https://www.tennessean.com/story/opinion/2017/10/29/free-last-escaping-cycle-drugs-and-prison/106717620/.
7. Lucas L. Johnson, "Crack in the Family," *Essence* (August 1992): 38.

ABOUT THE AUTHOR

Lucas L. Johnson II, a Memphis, Tennessee, native, is a former reporter for the Associated Press where he worked for twenty-four years. His news coverage included politics, education, health care, religion, and entertainment. One of his most notable stories was the discovery of an old audio reel in a Chattanooga attic that contained an unheard recording of Dr. Martin Luther King Jr. He also wrote a follow-up story in which magician David Copperfield purchased the newly discovered audiotape and donated it to the National Civil Rights Muscum in Memphis. Lucas is a freelance writer and communications strategist, and he lives in Nashville.